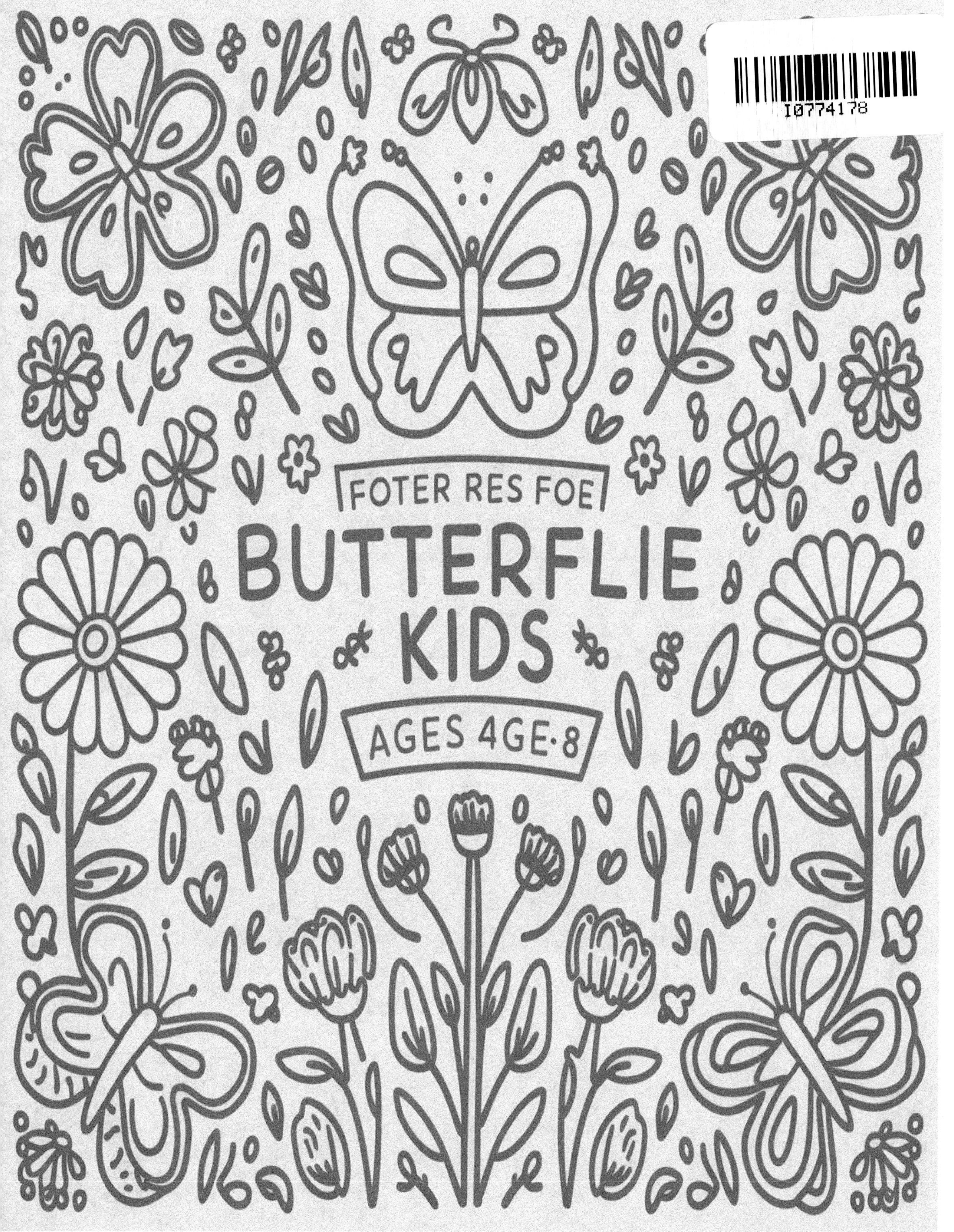
FOTER RES FOE
BUTTERFLIE
KIDS
AGES 4GE·8

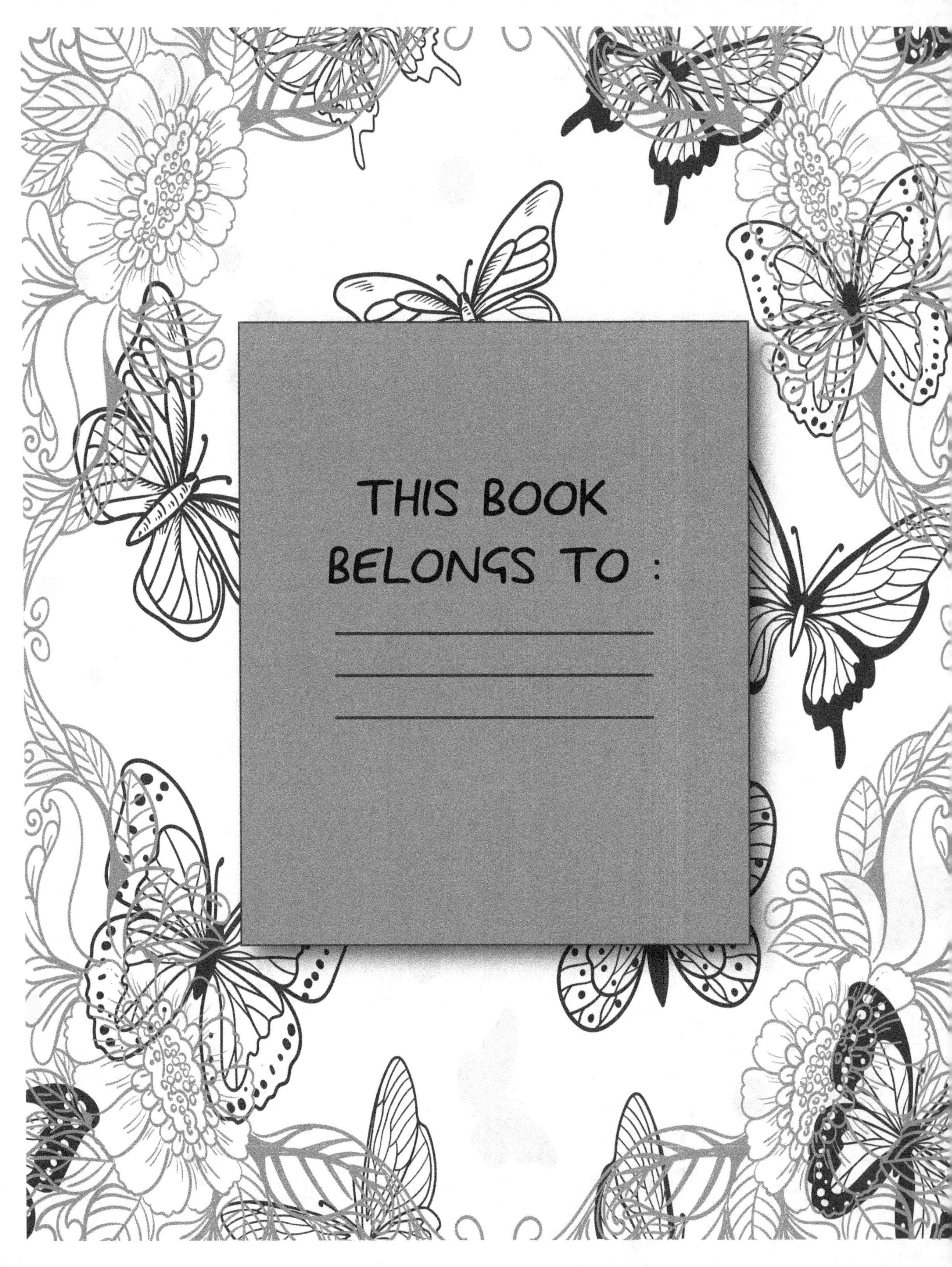
THIS BOOK
BELONGS TO :

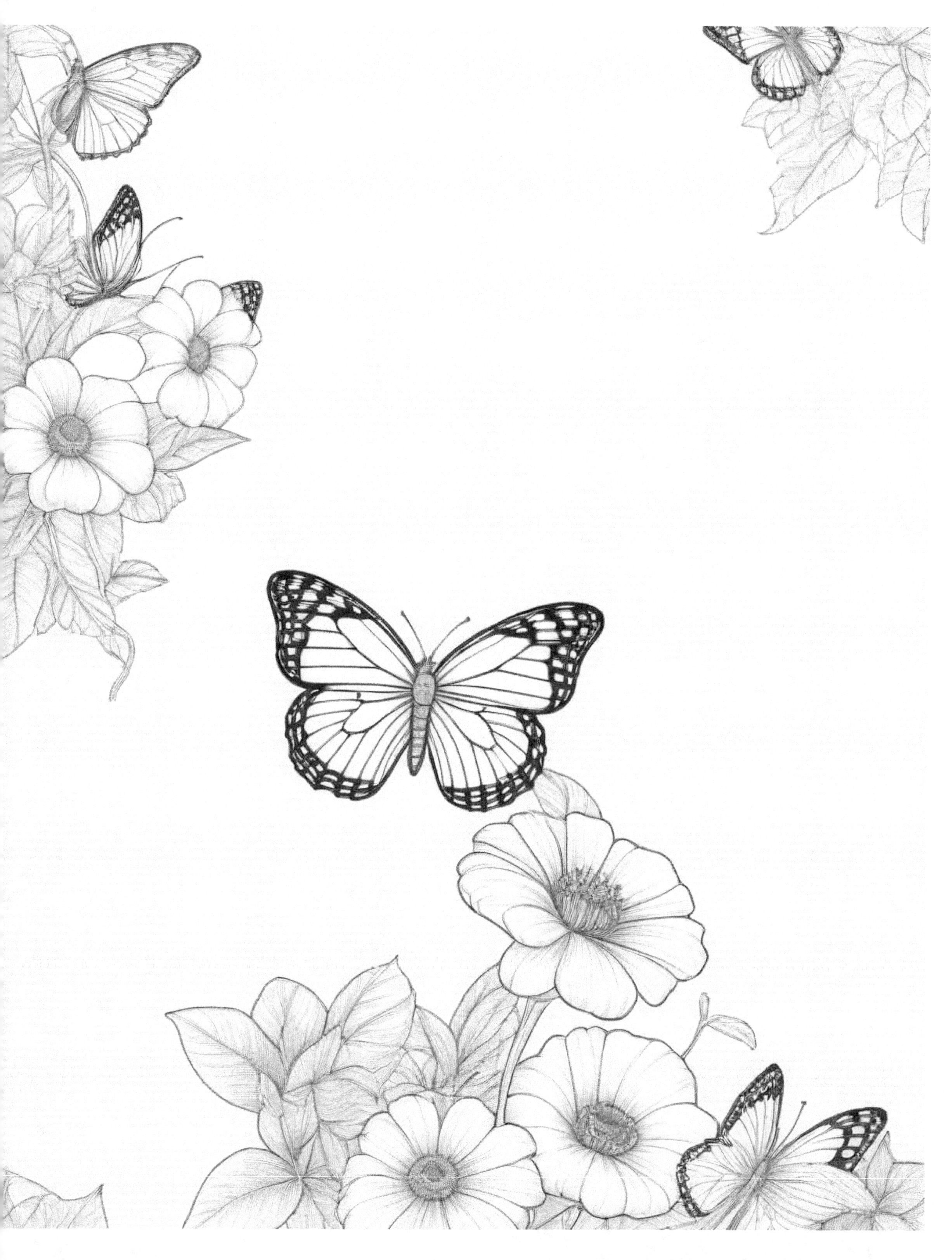

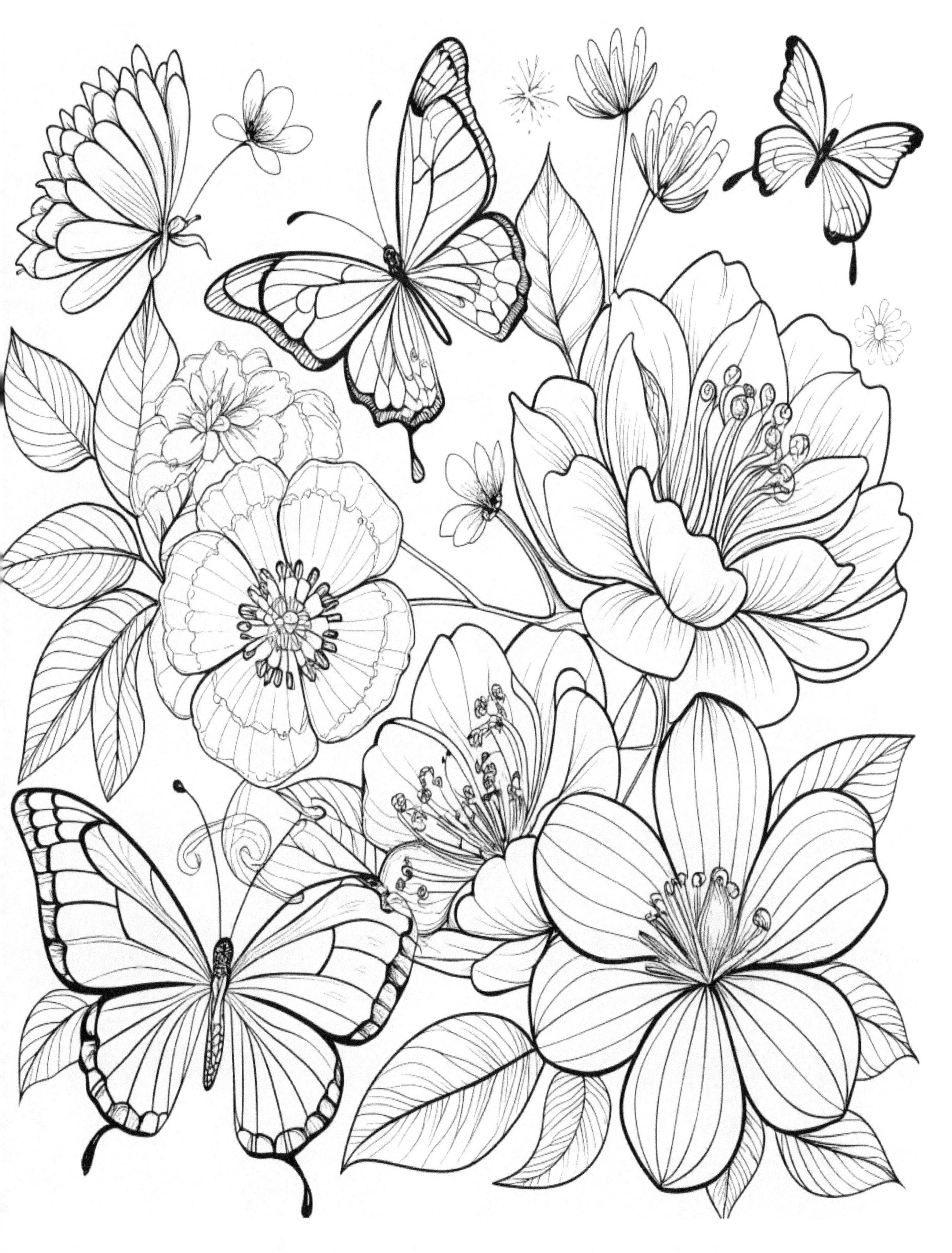

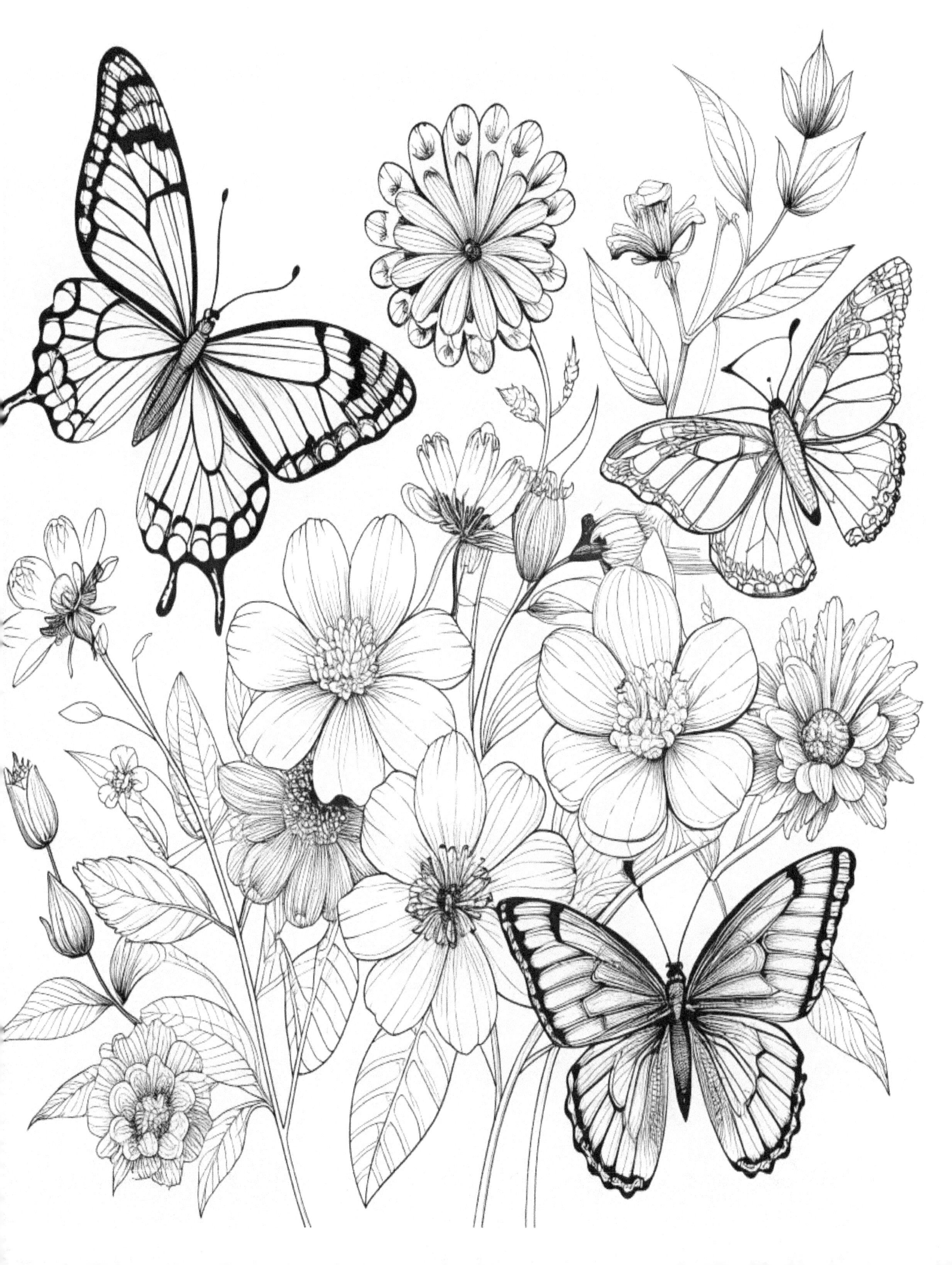

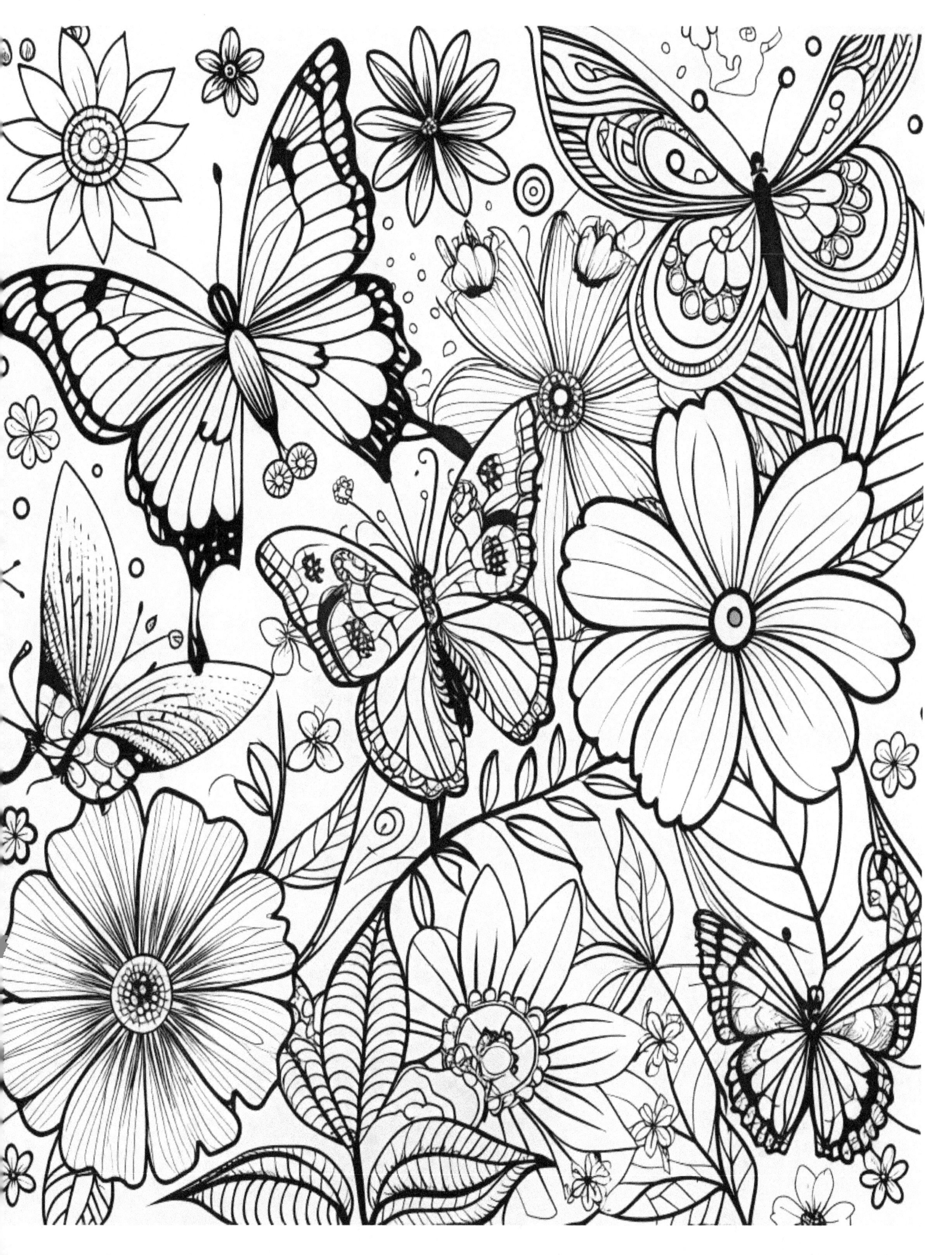

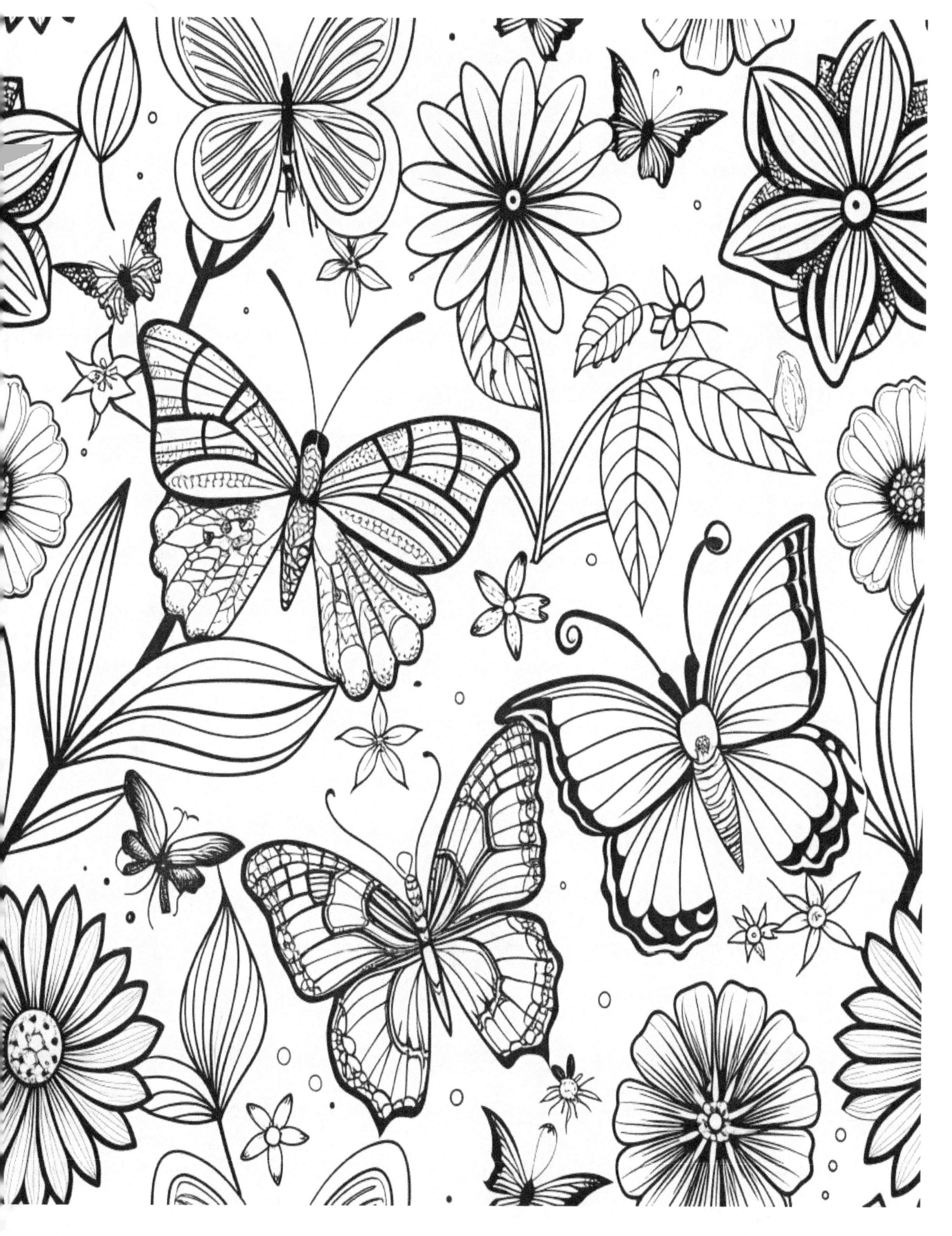

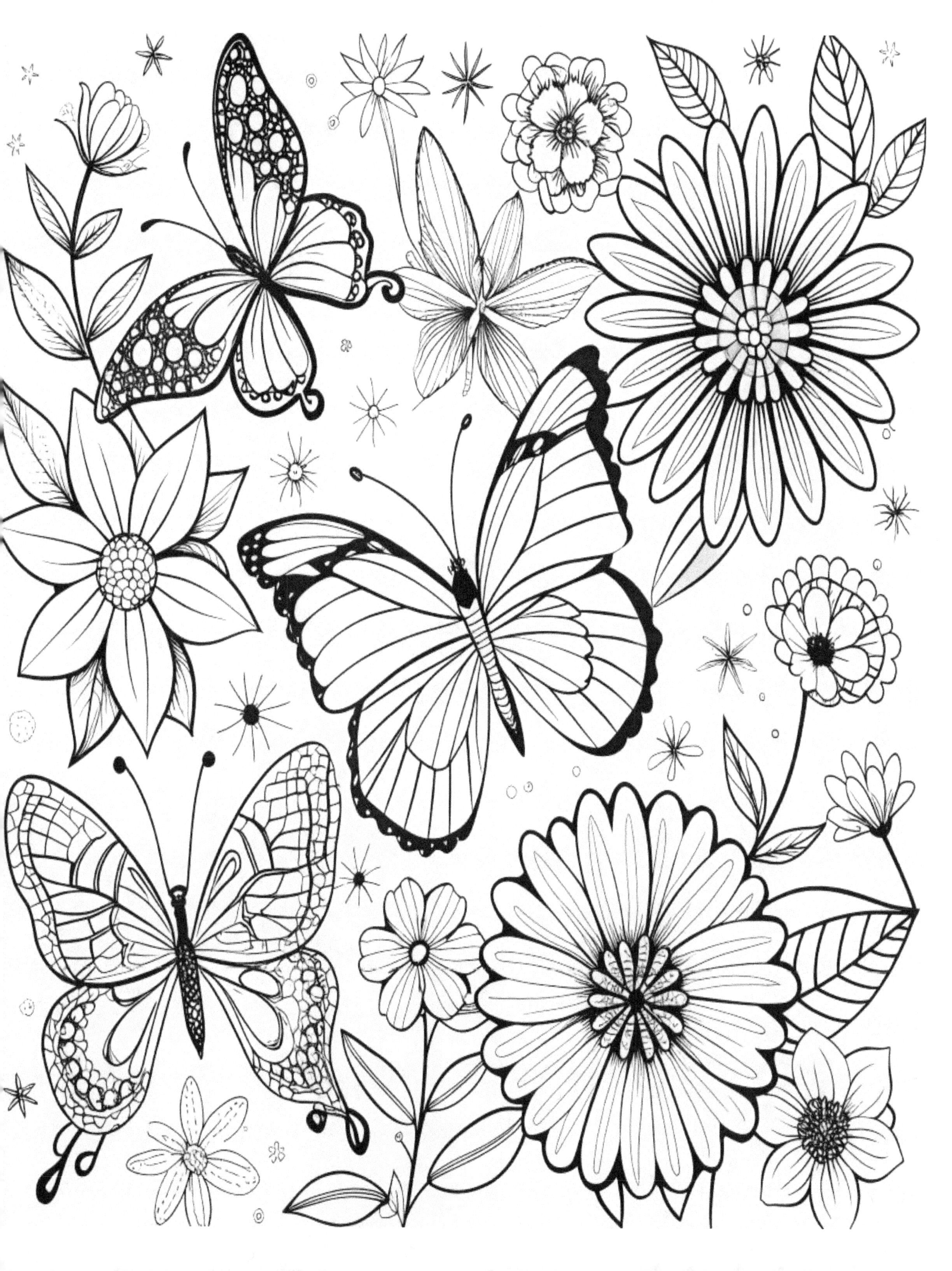

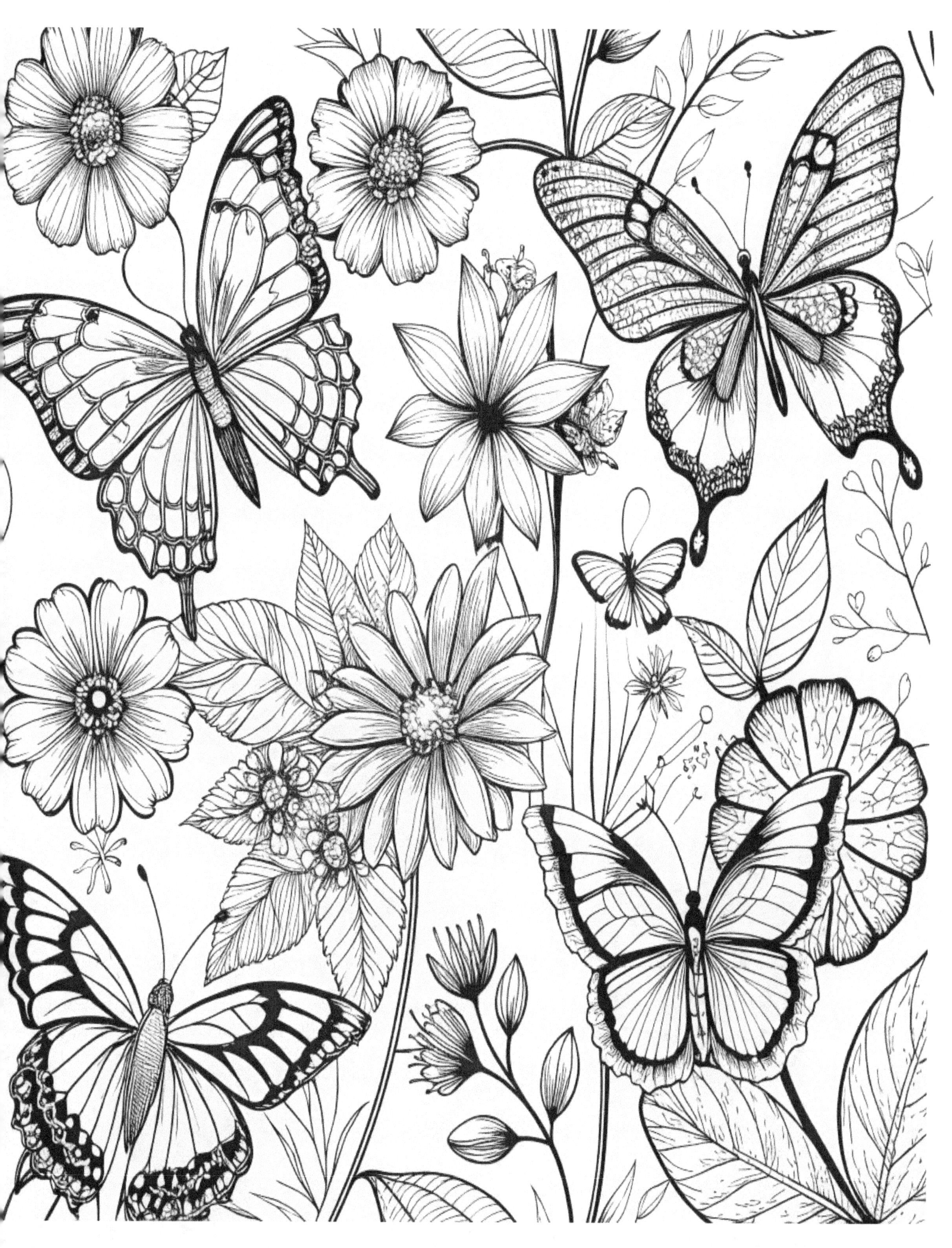

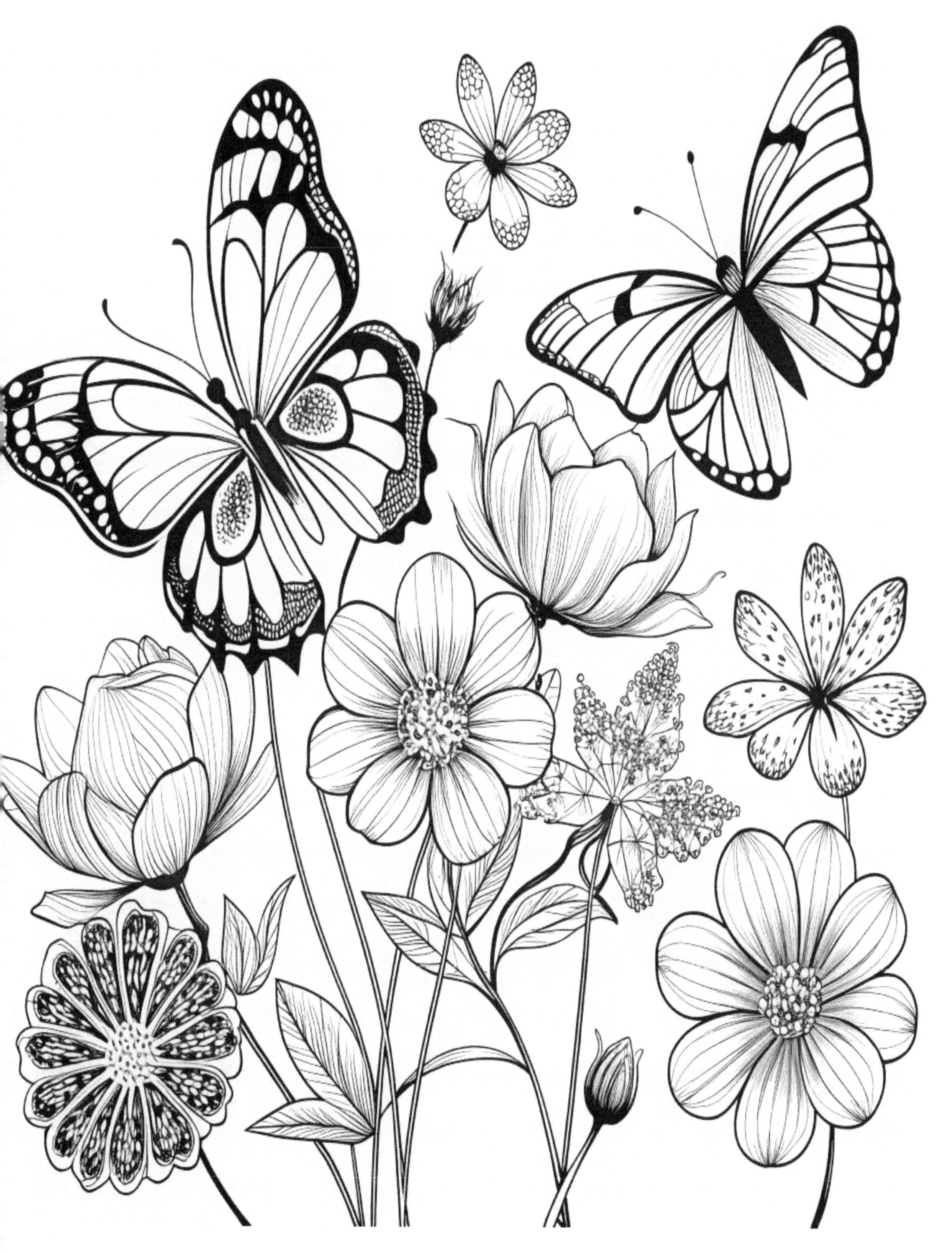

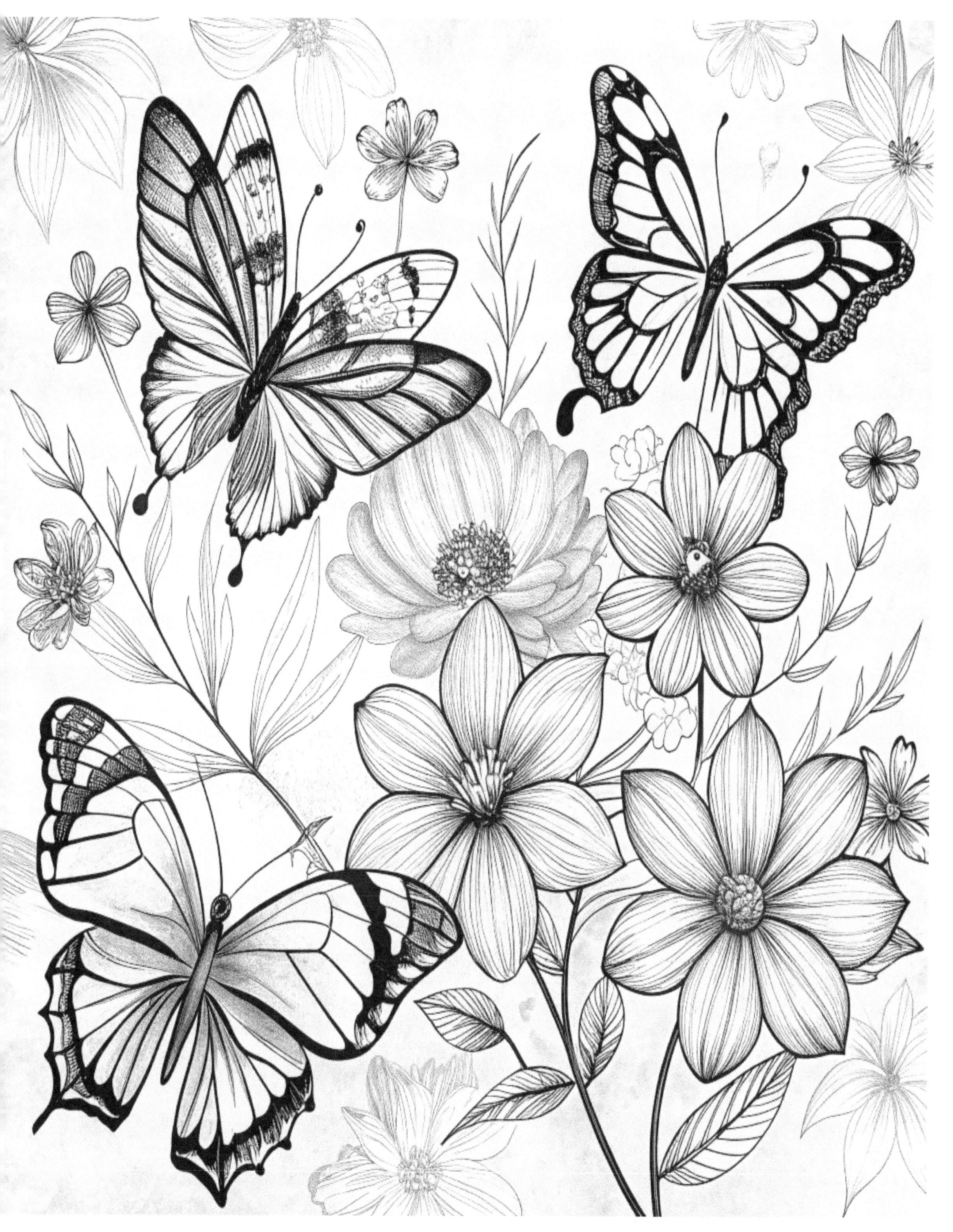

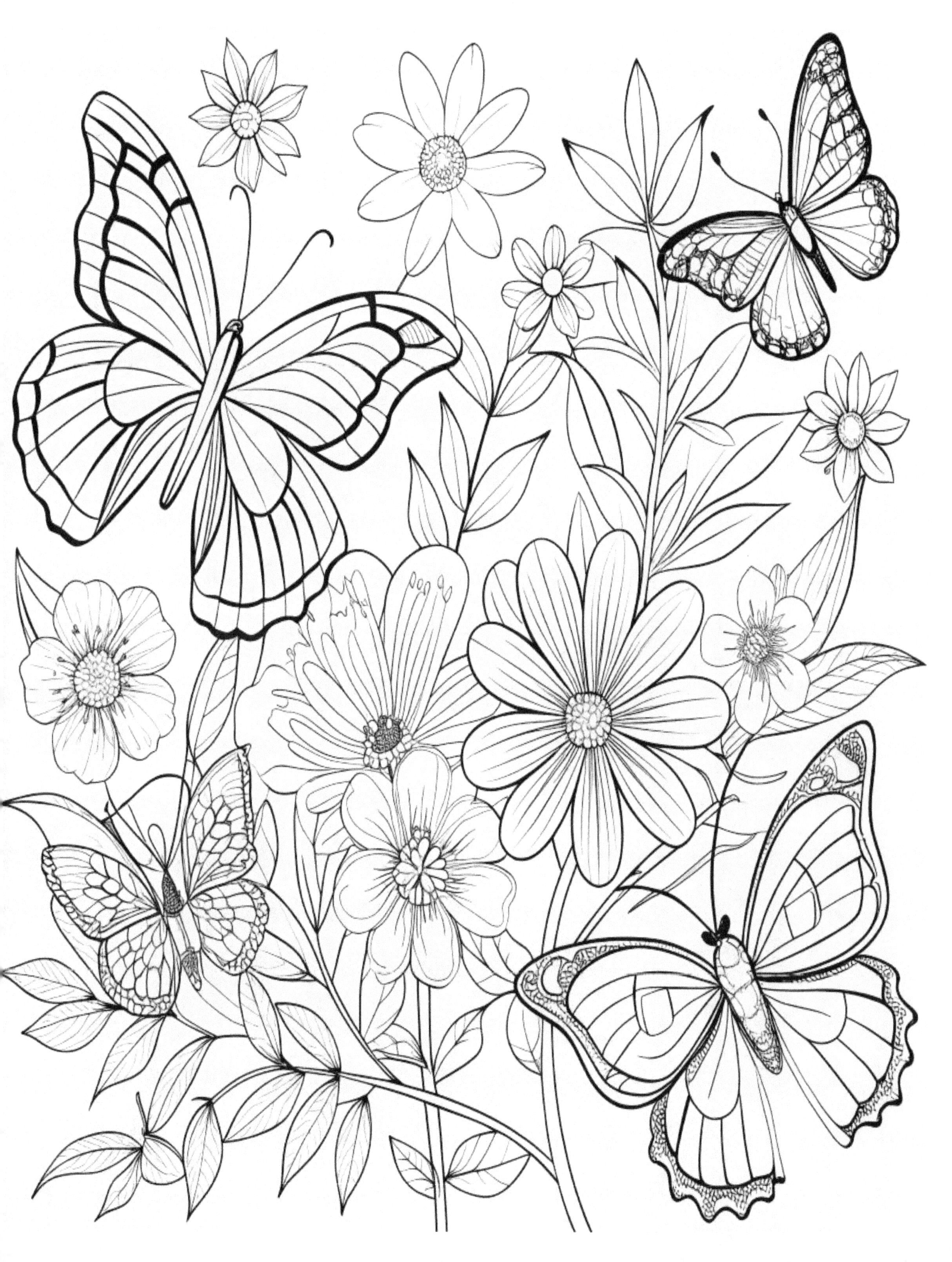

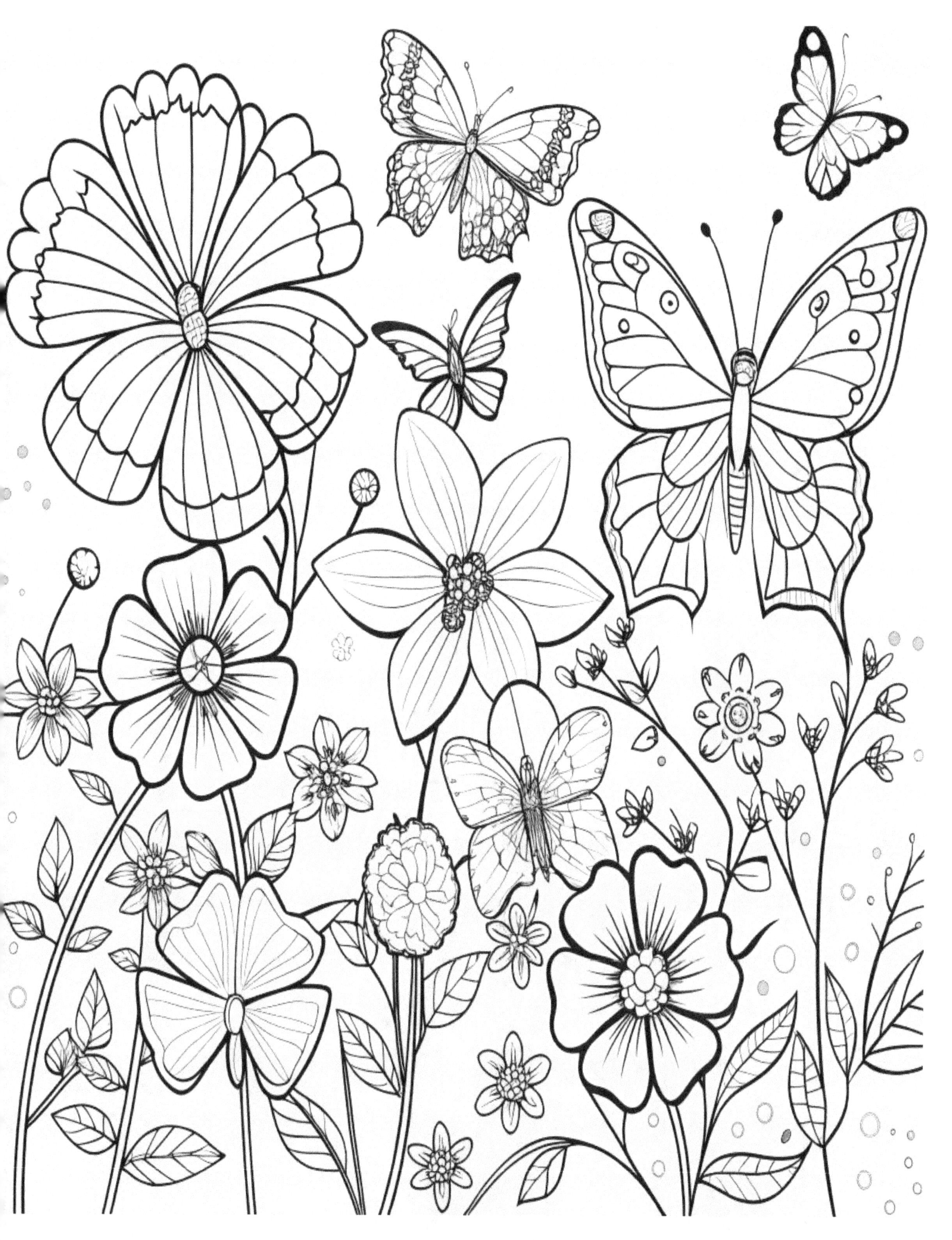

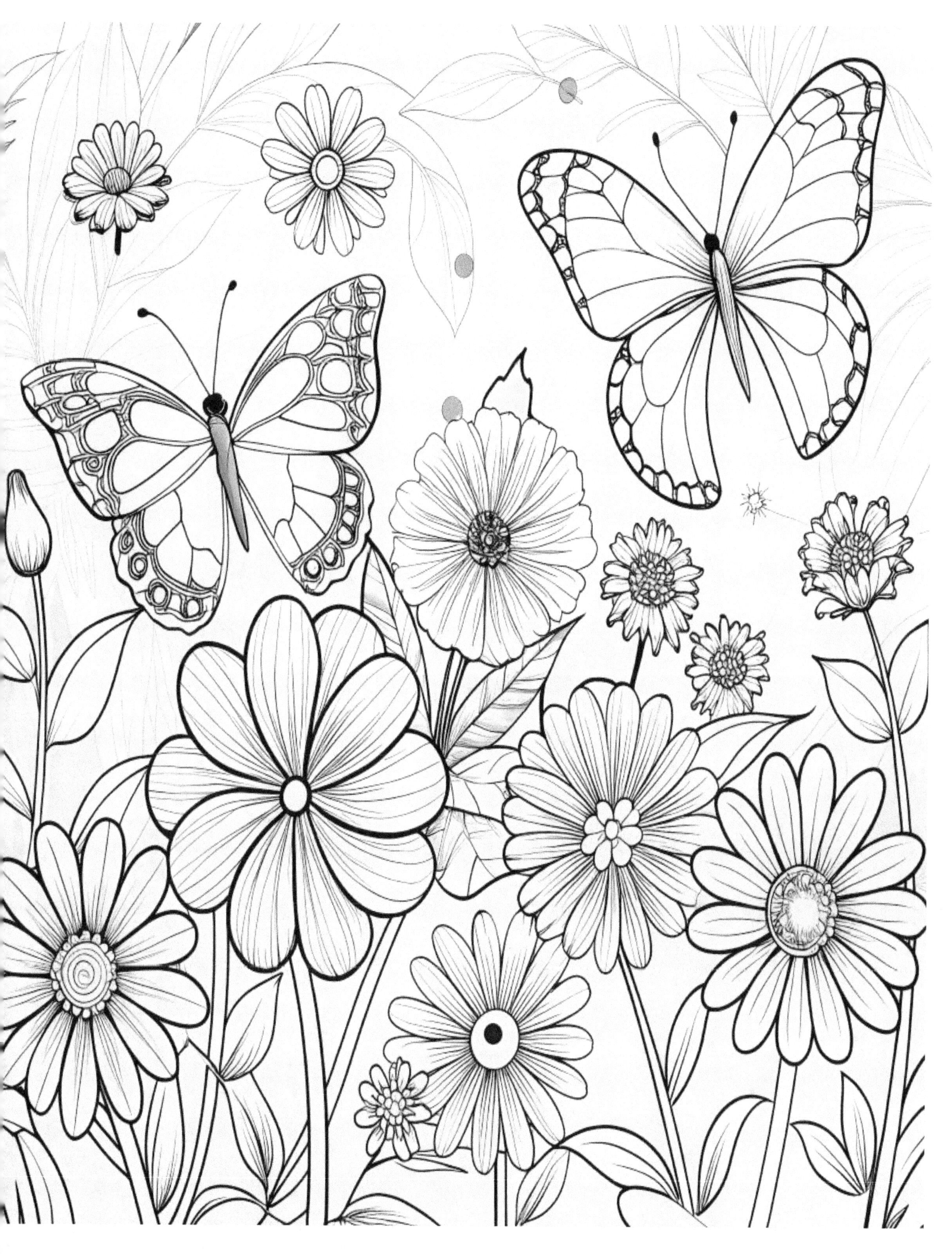

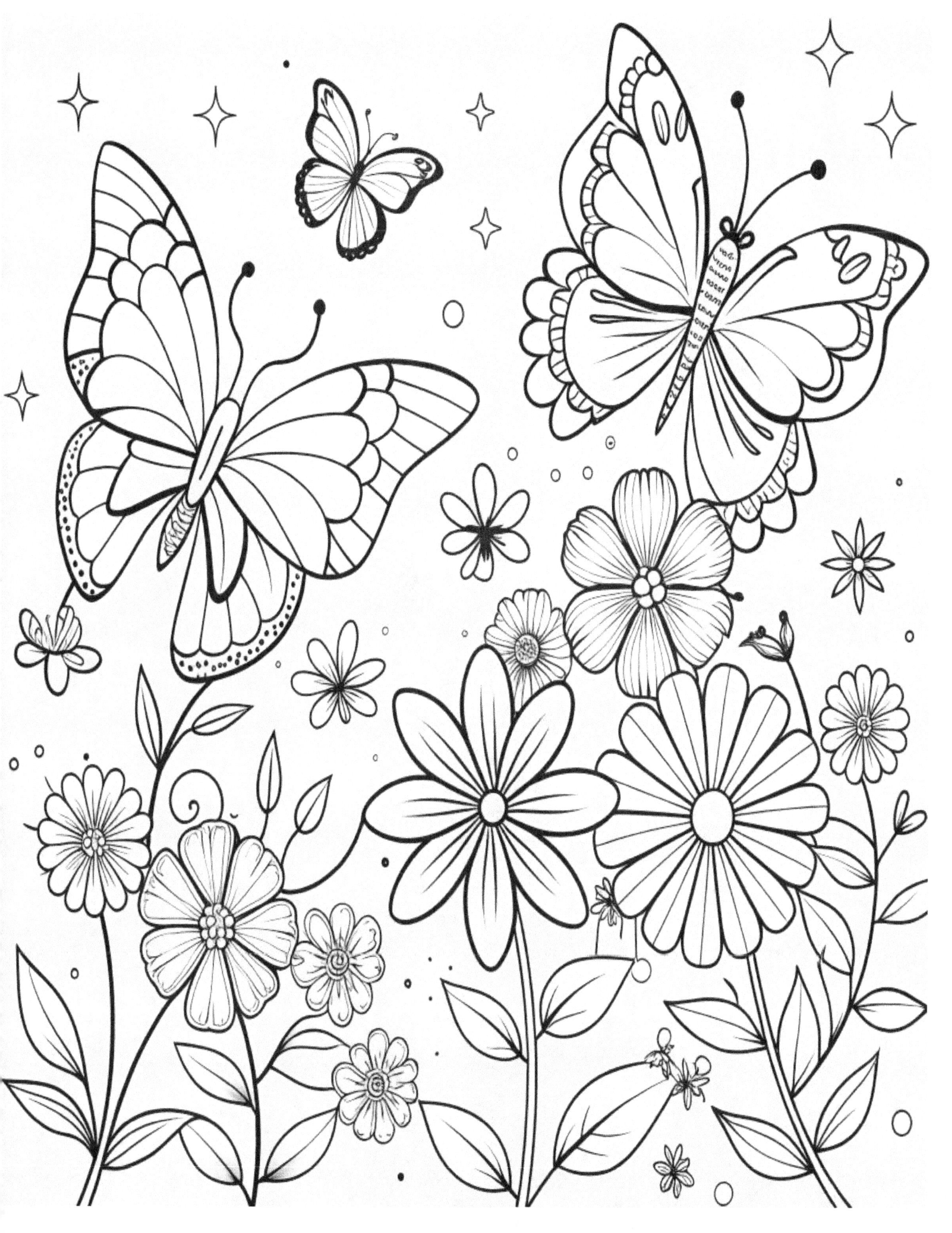

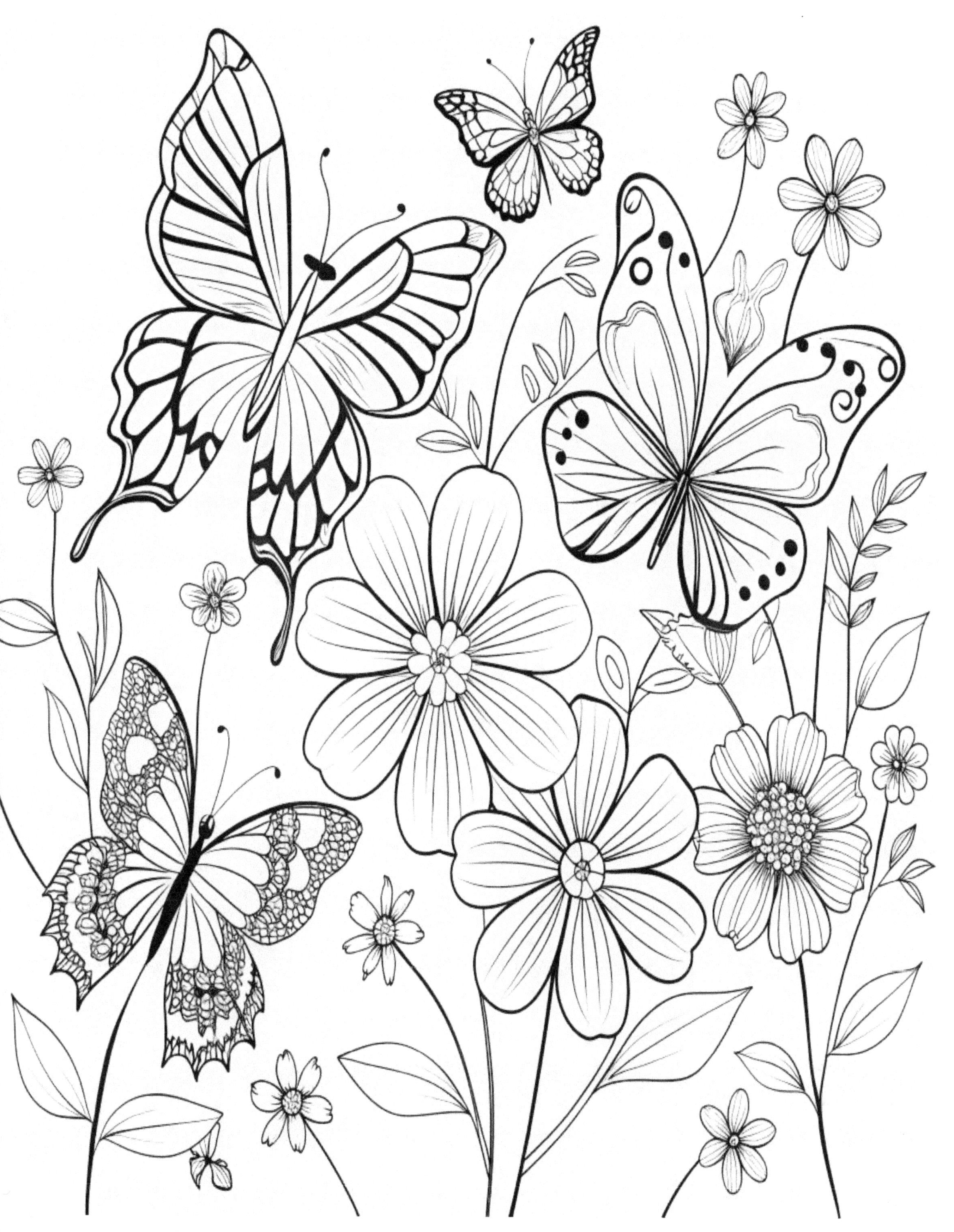

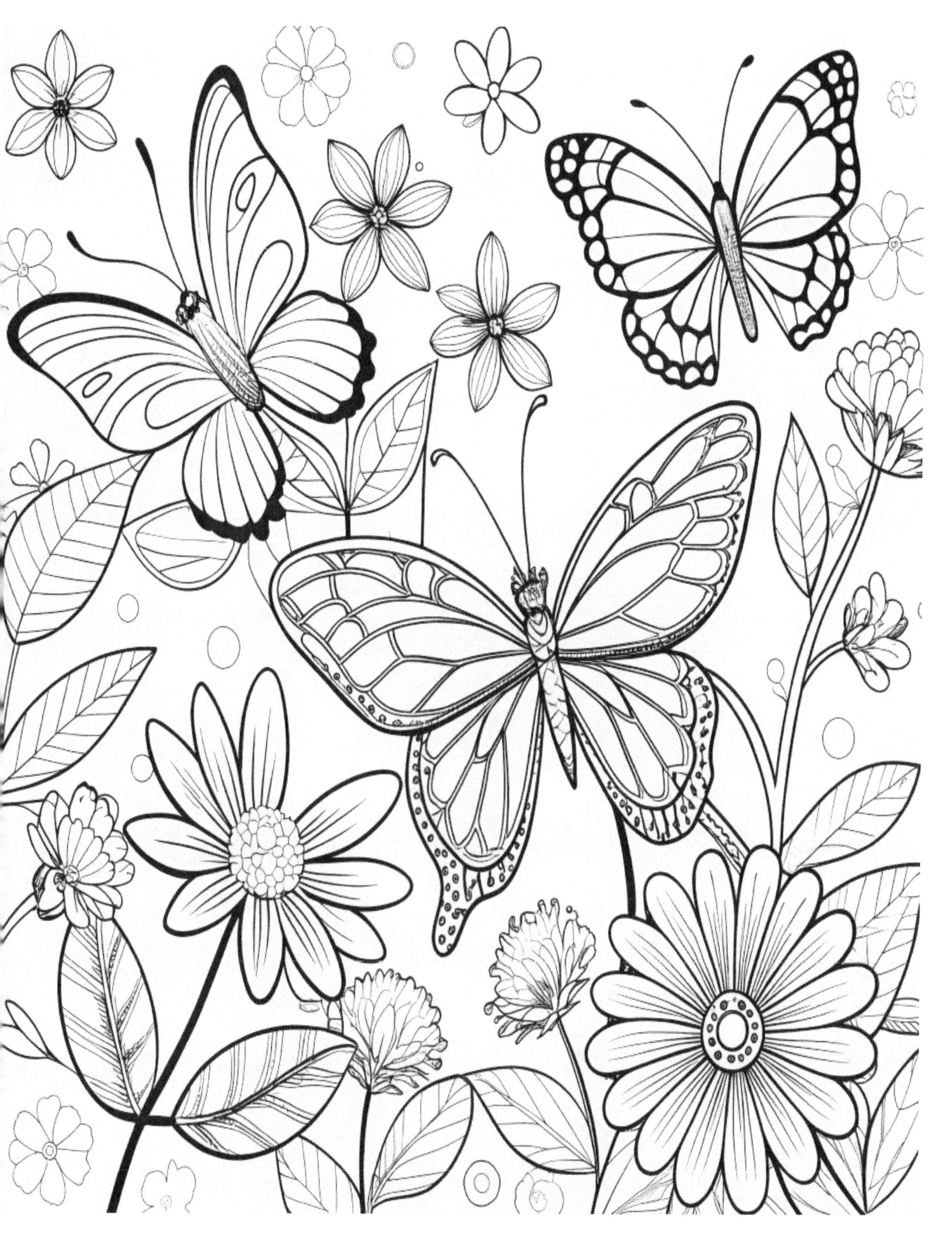

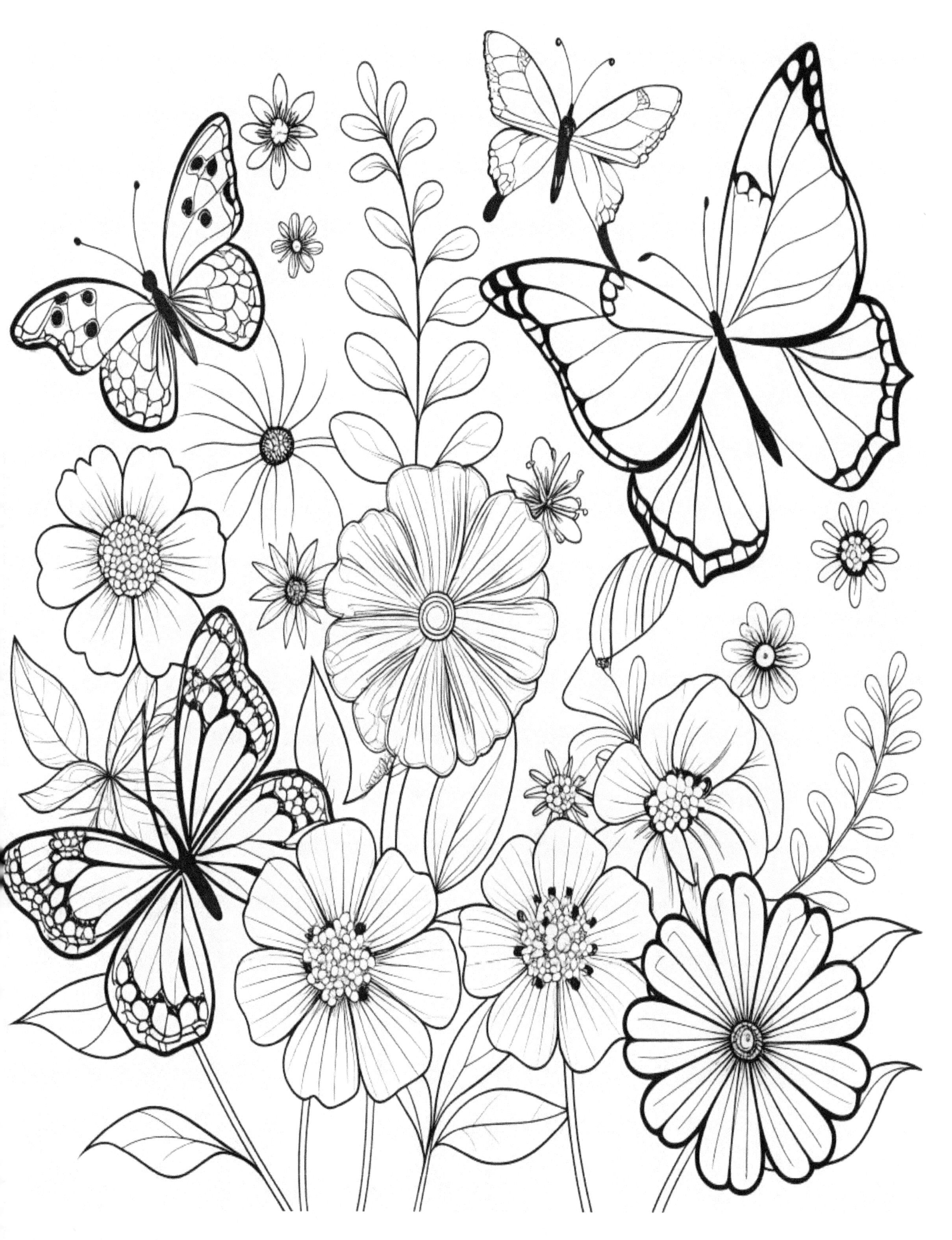

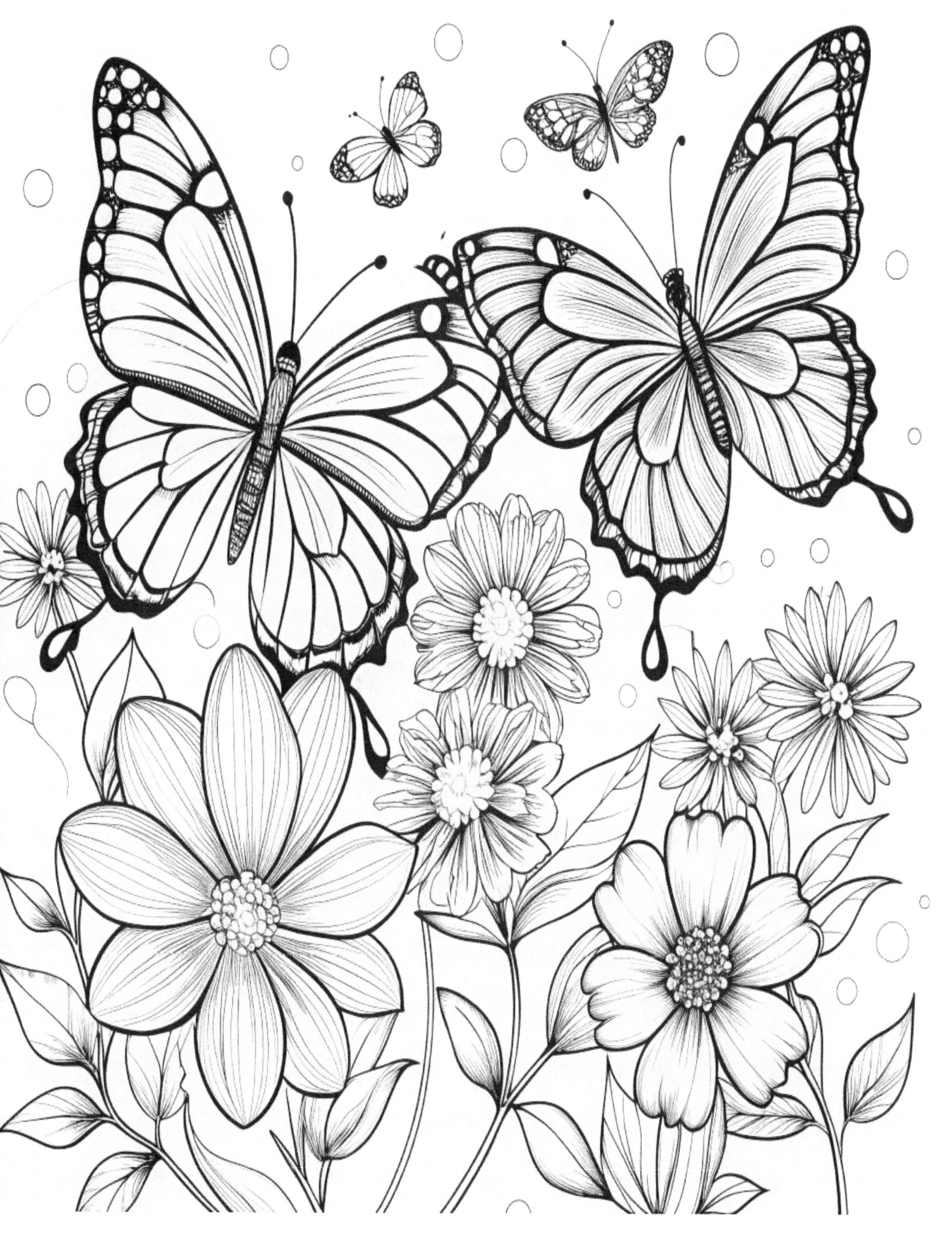

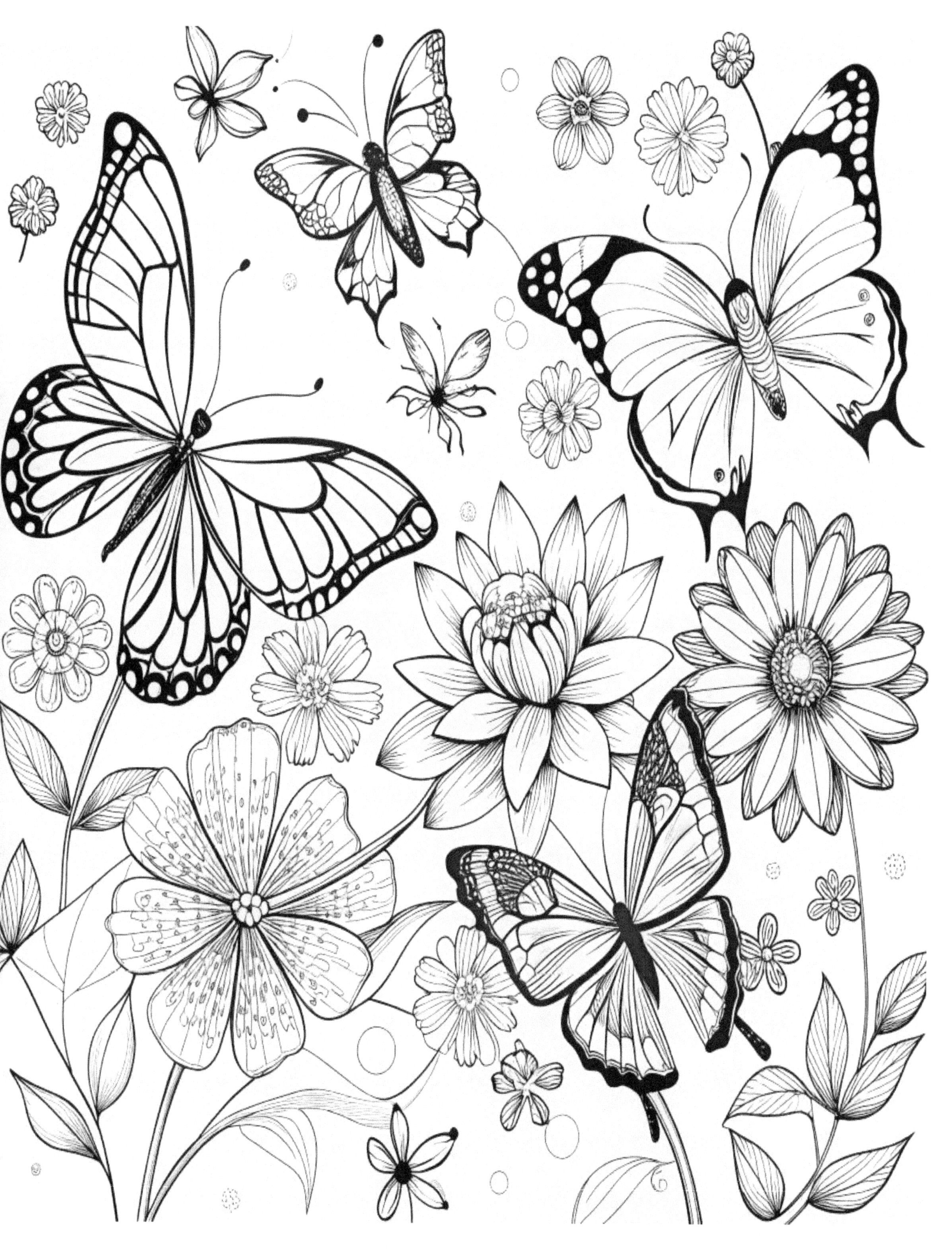

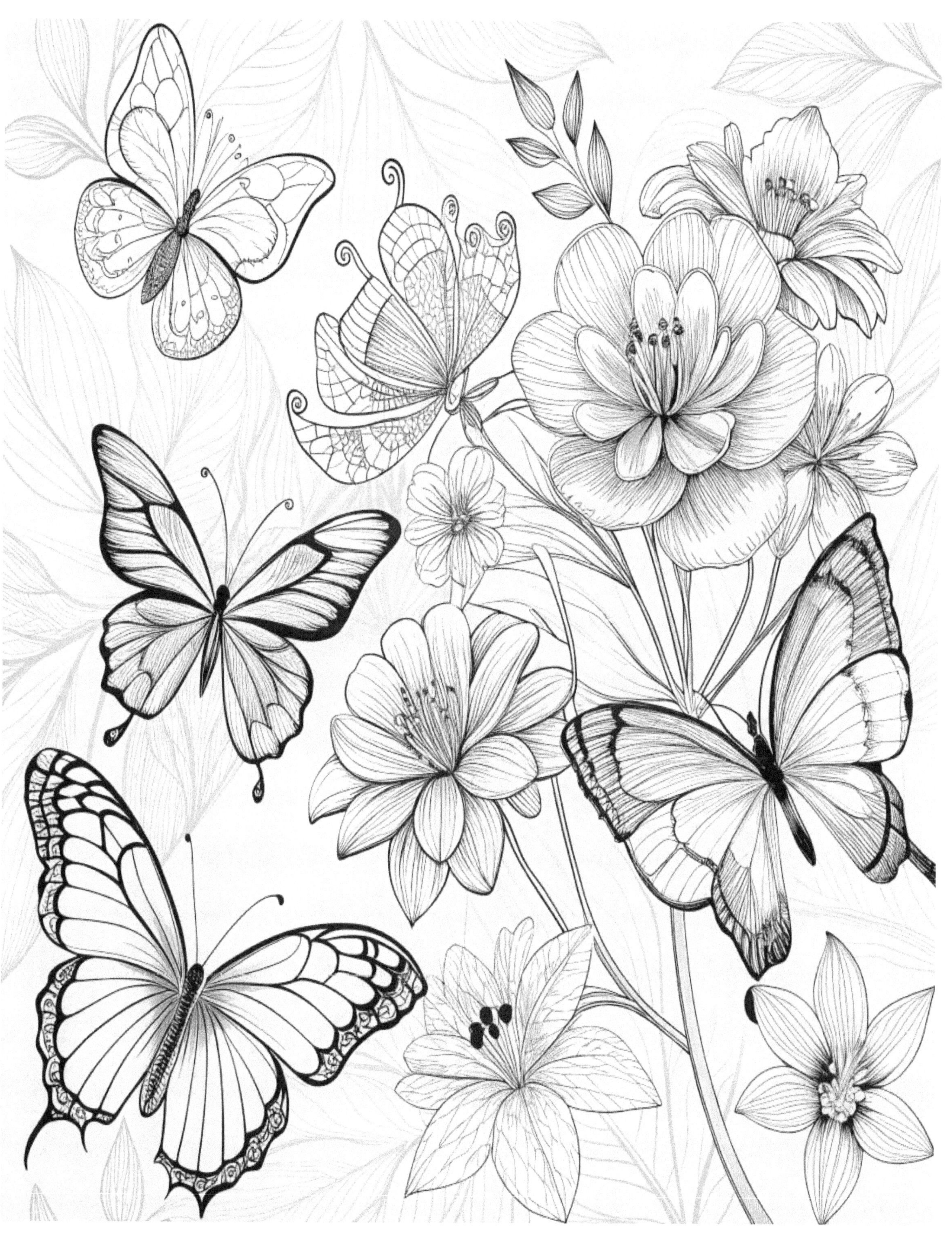

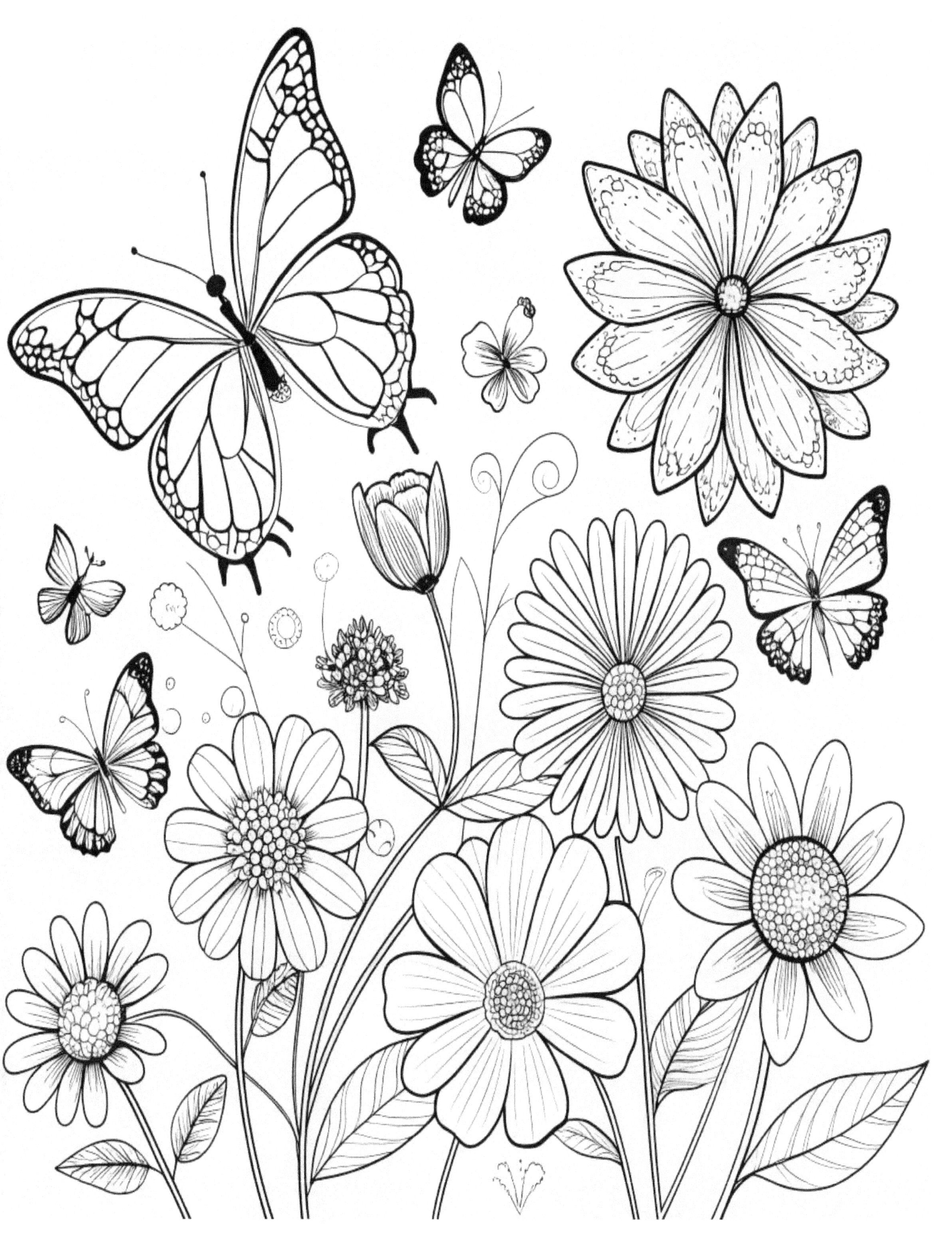

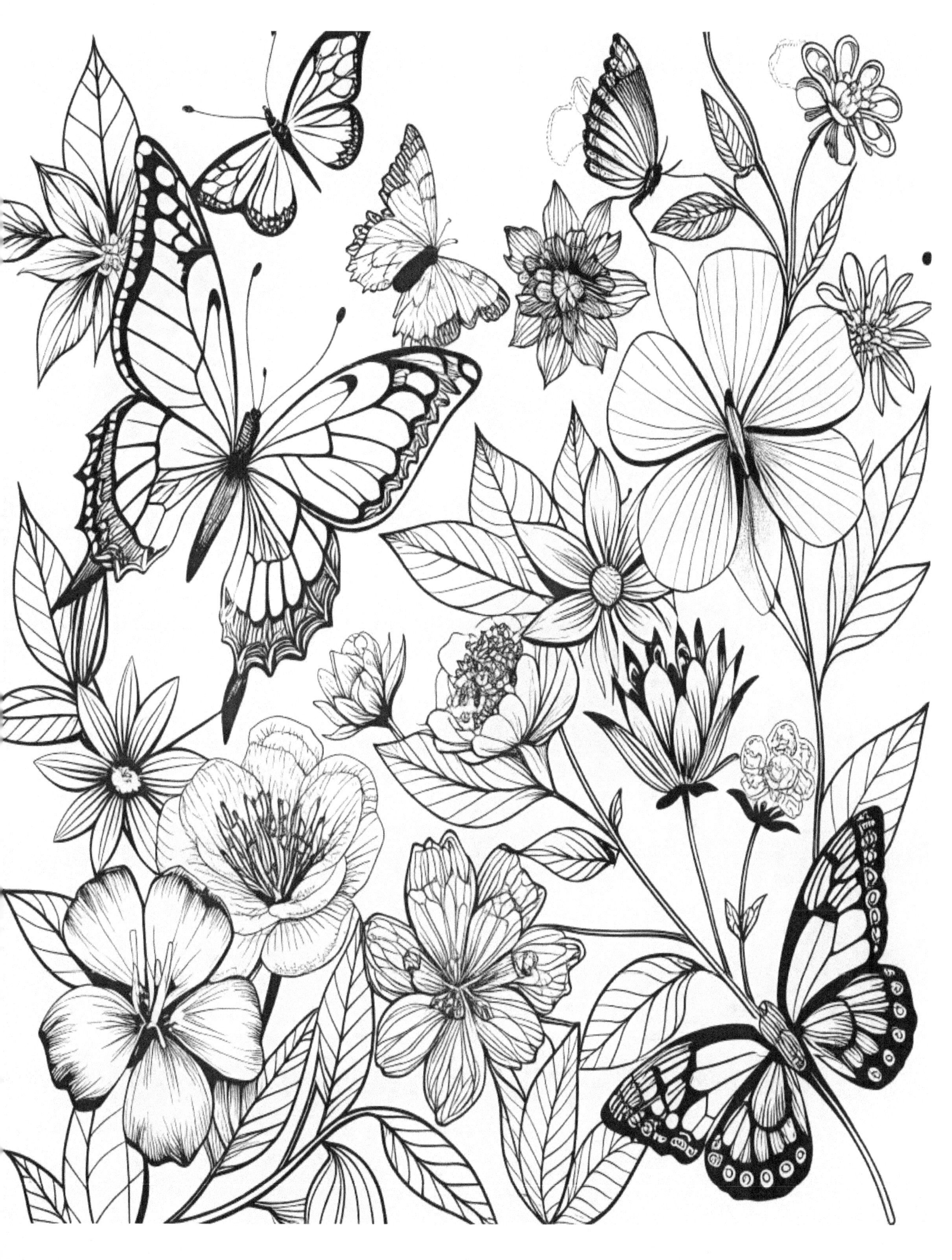

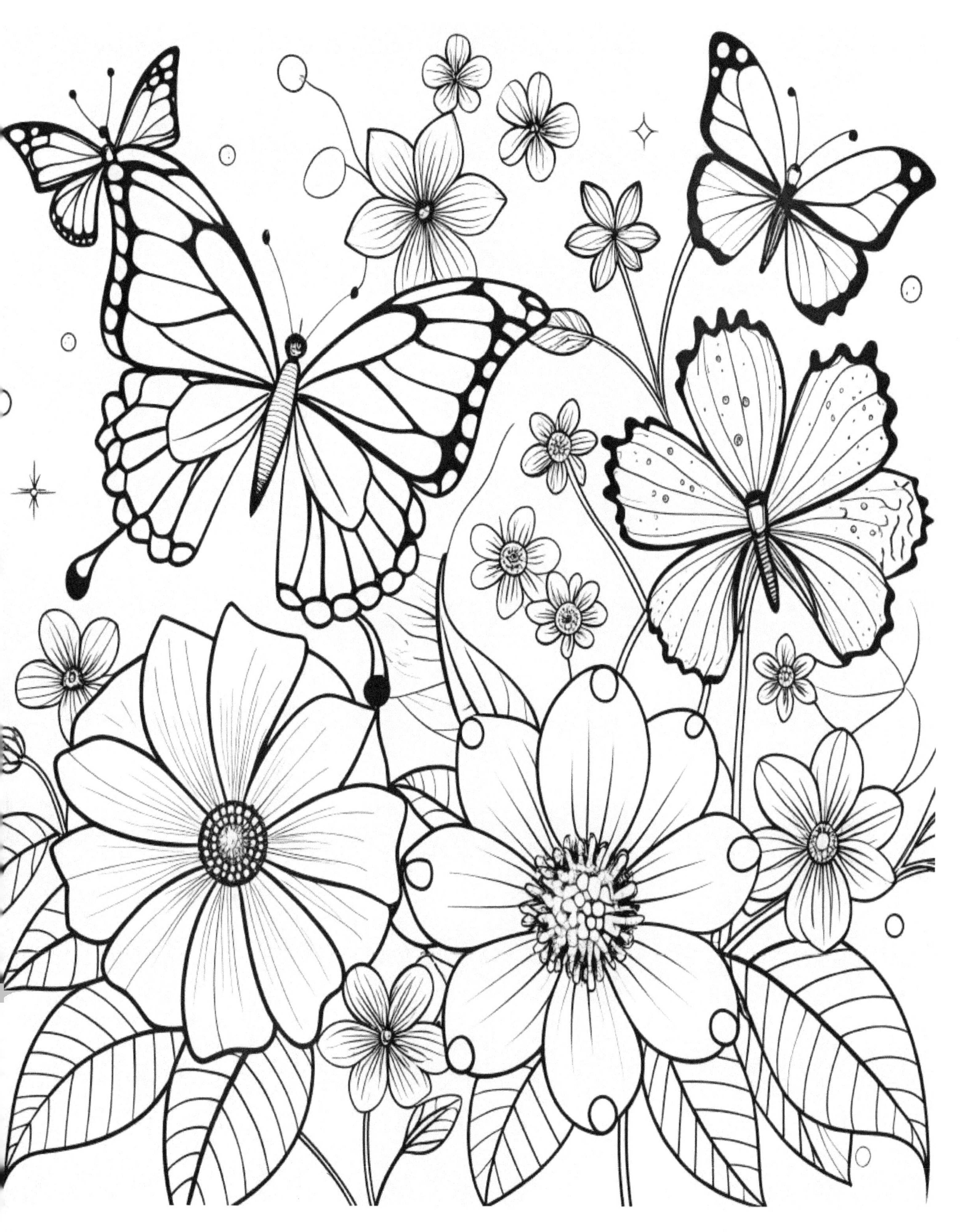

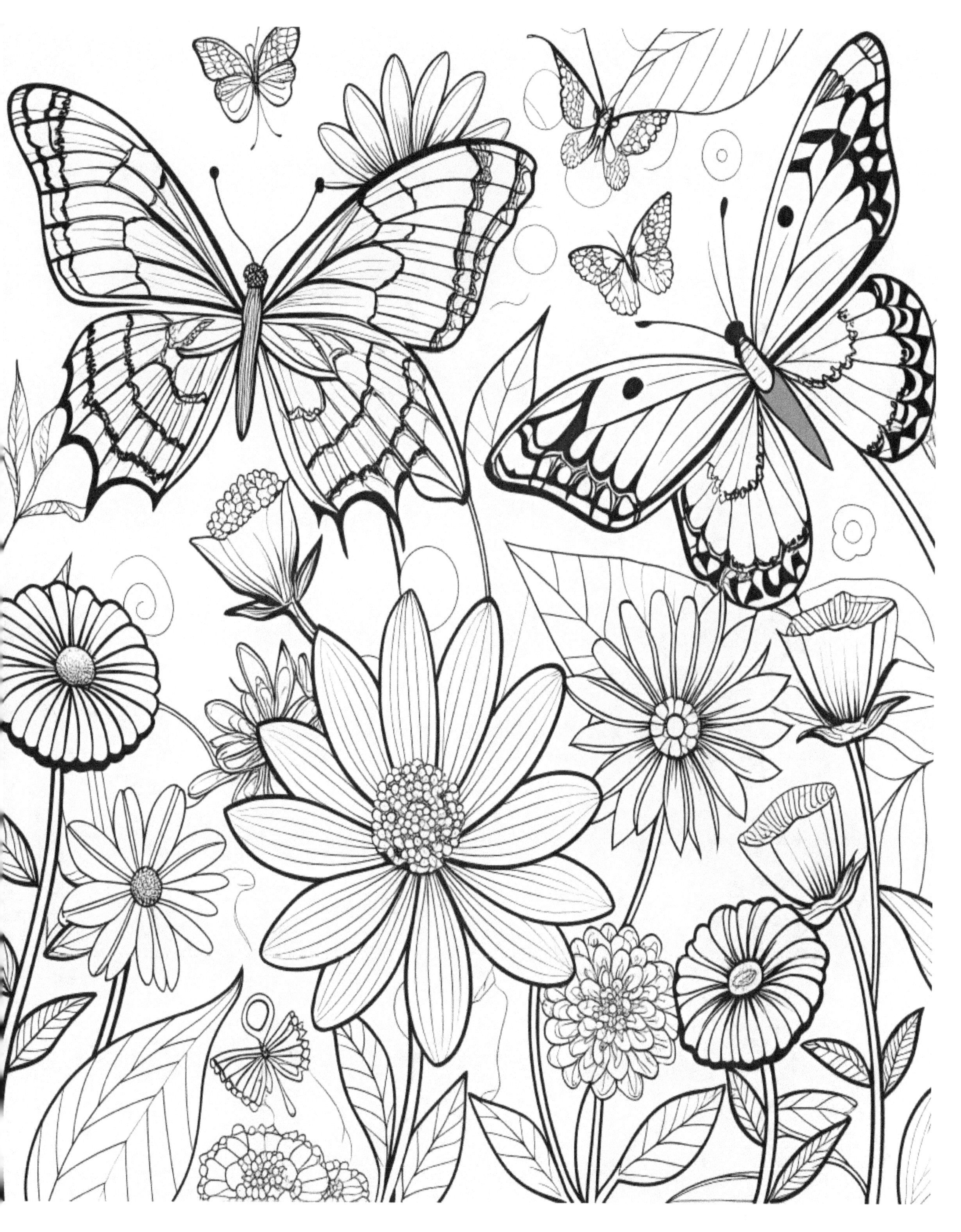

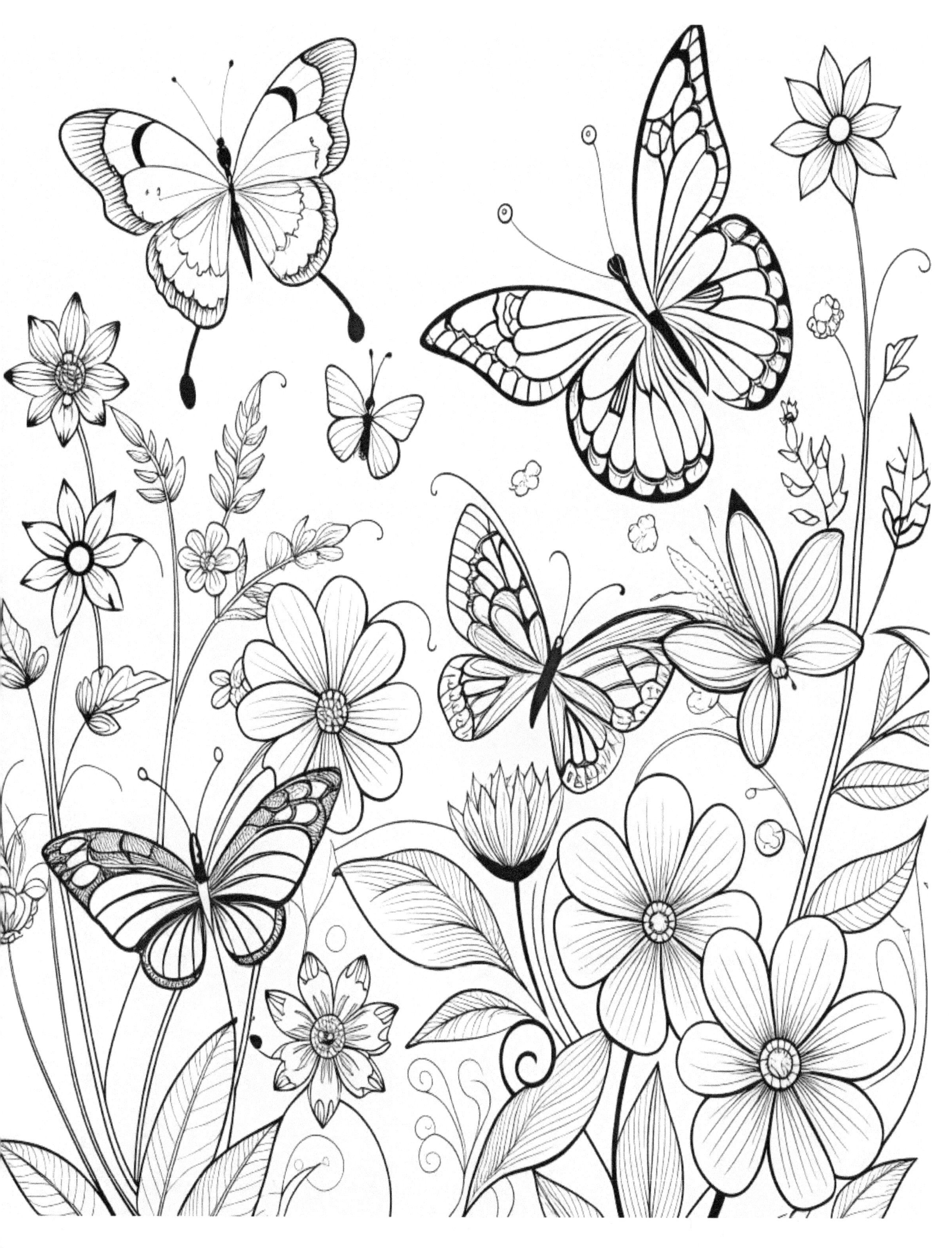

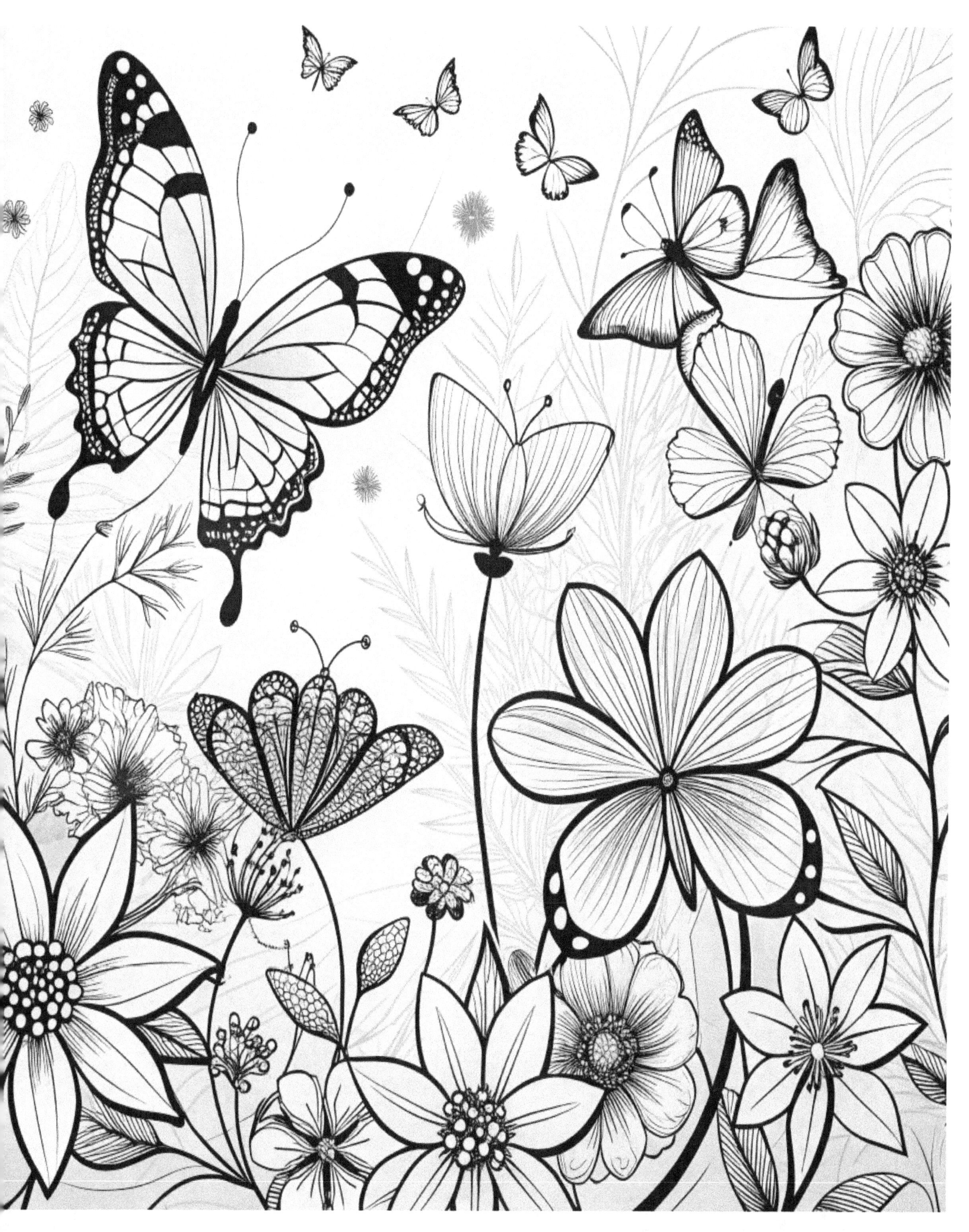

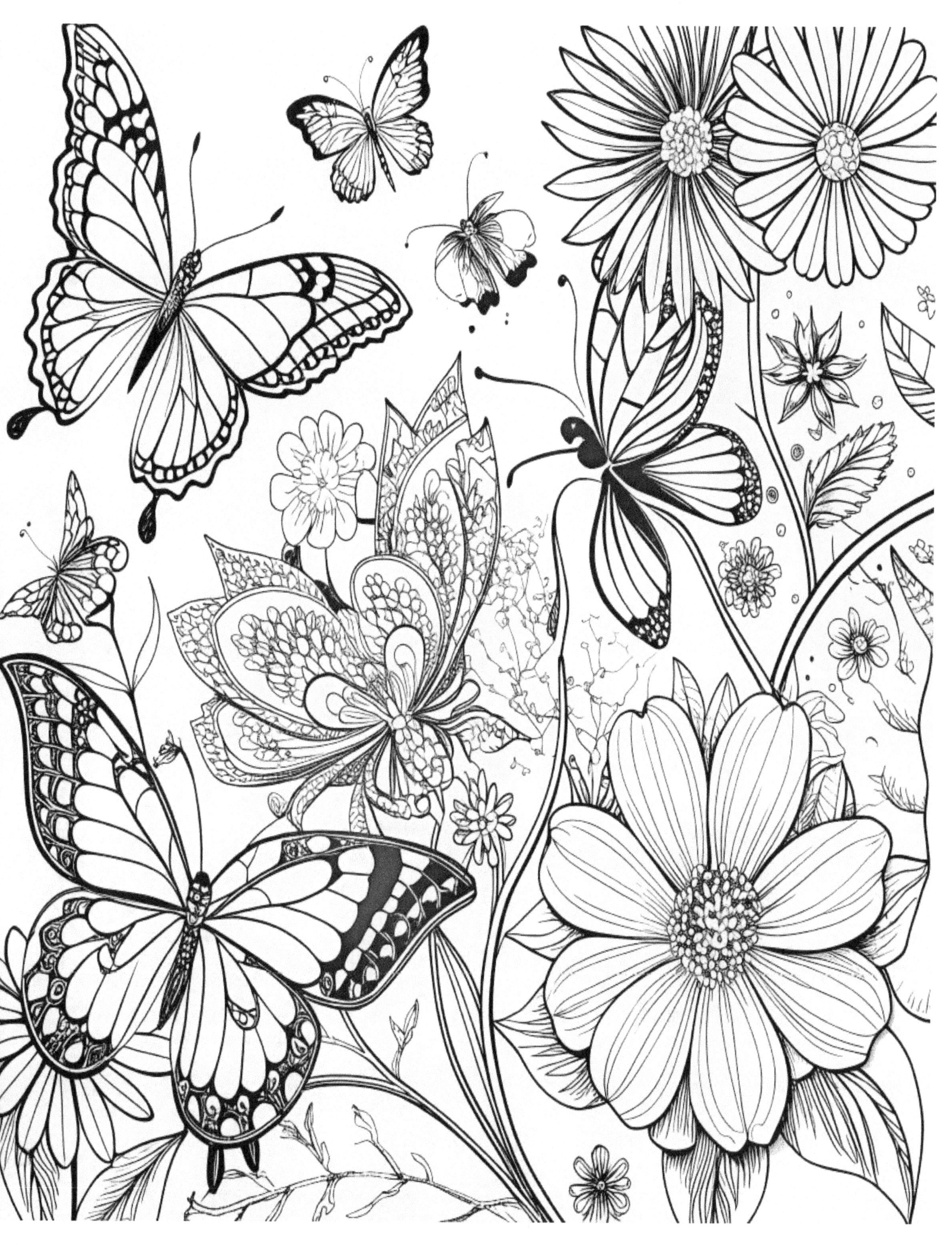

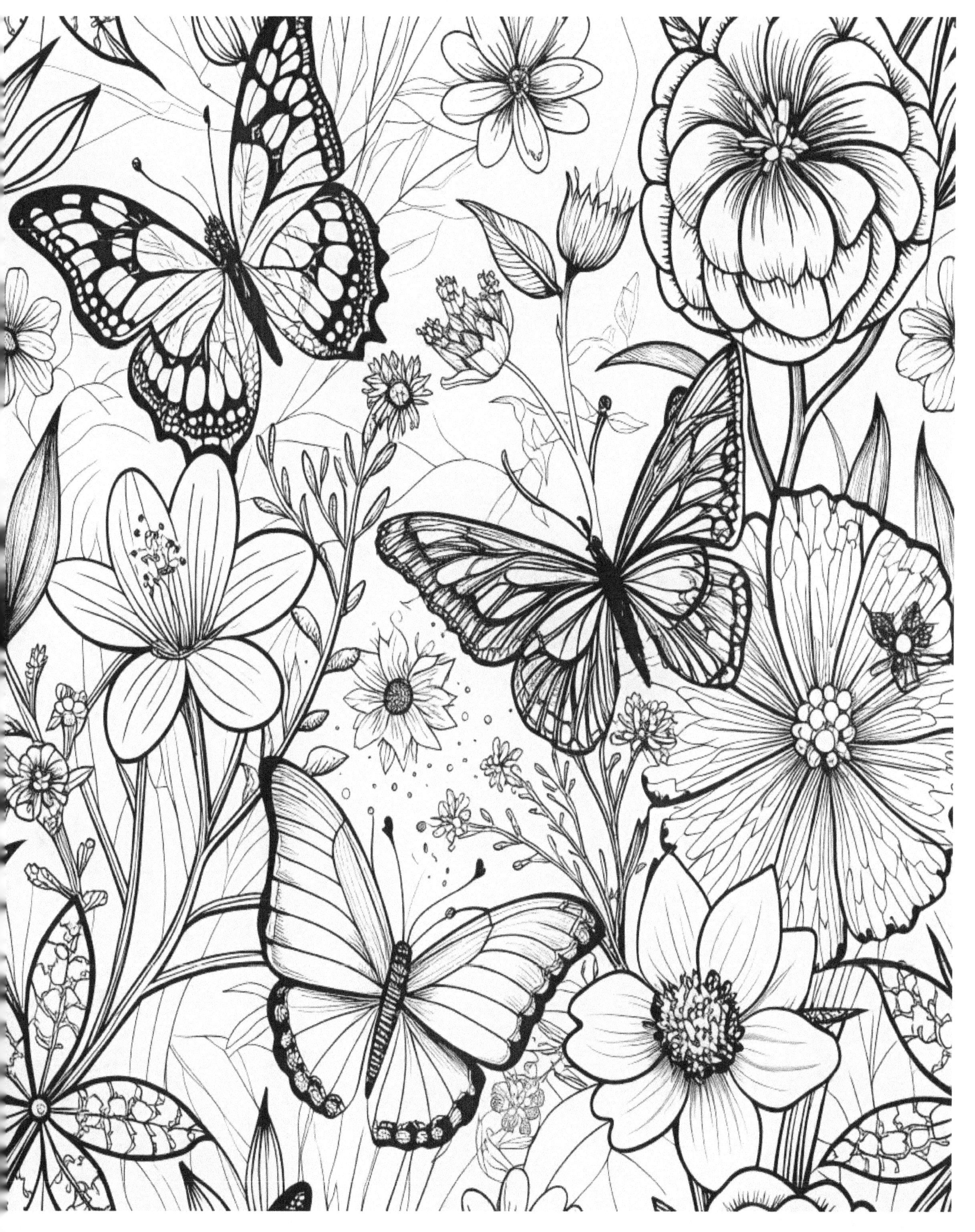

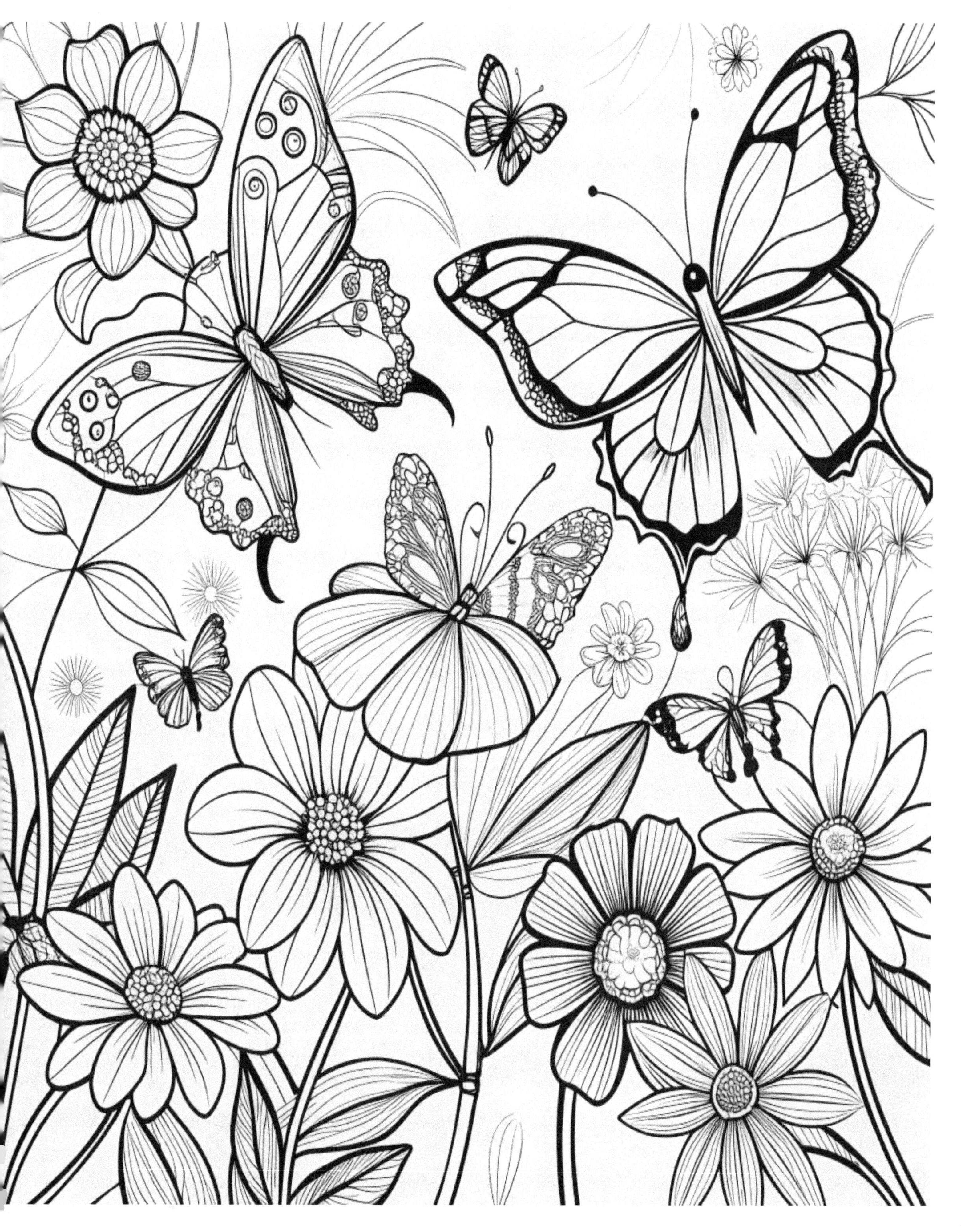

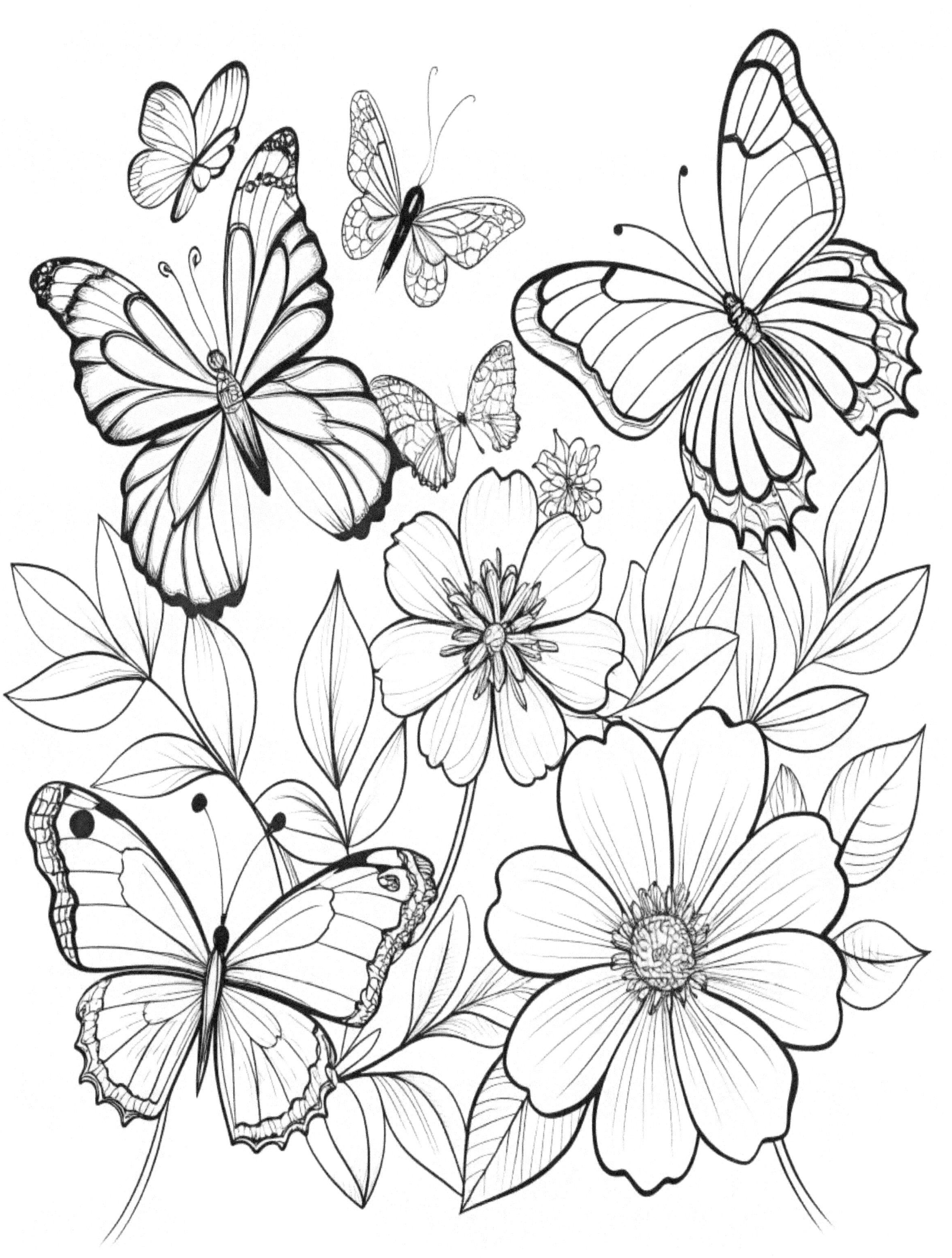

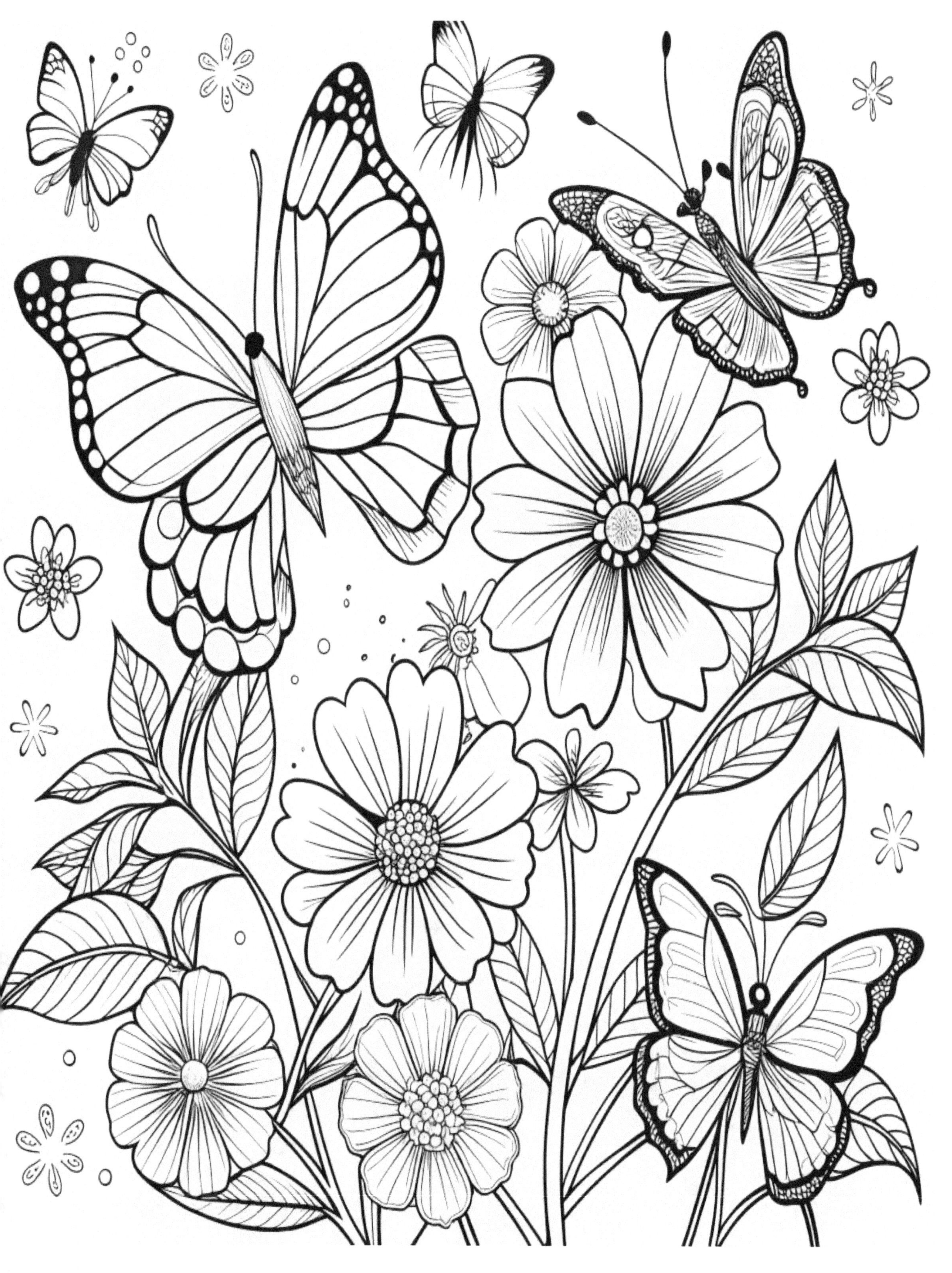

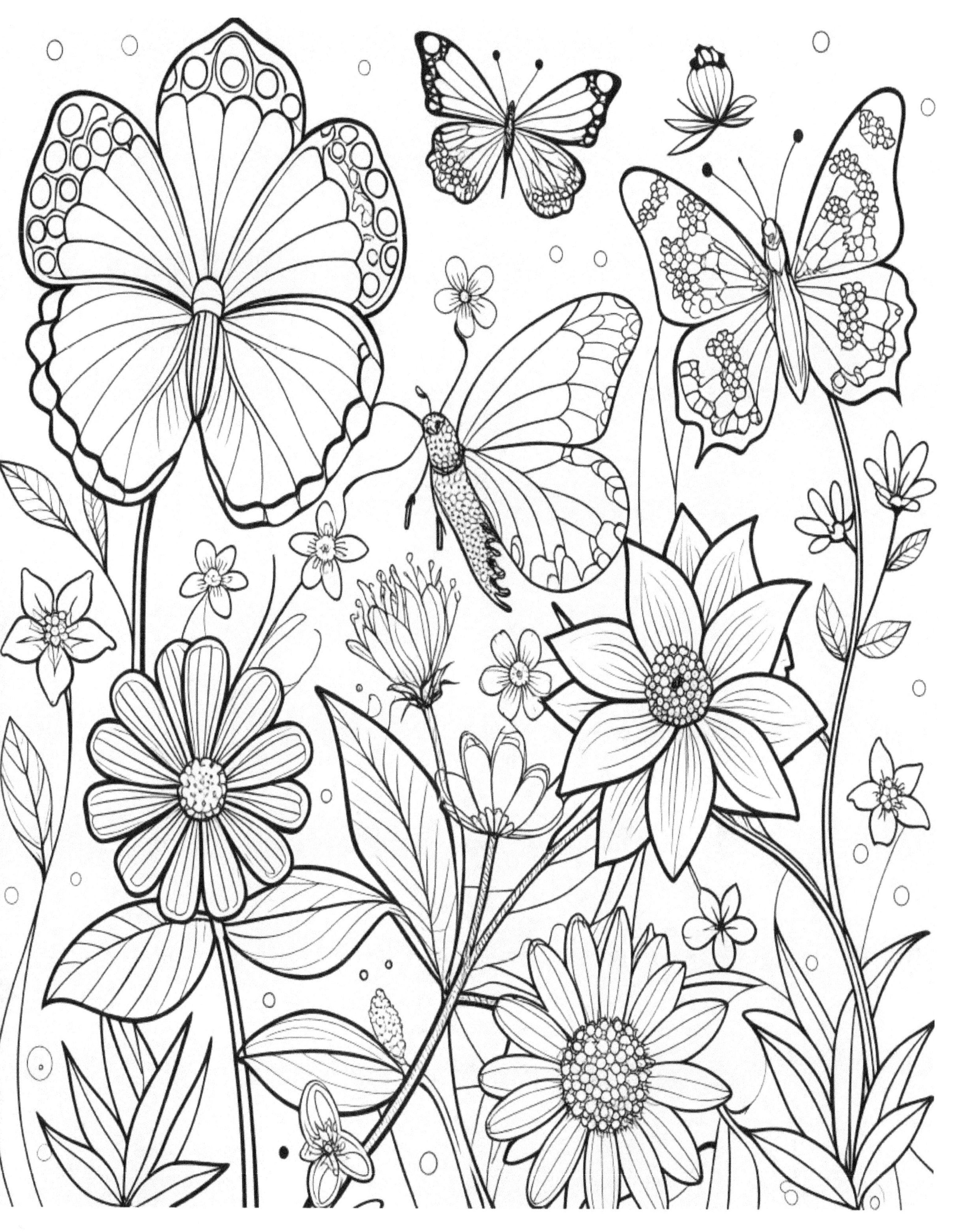

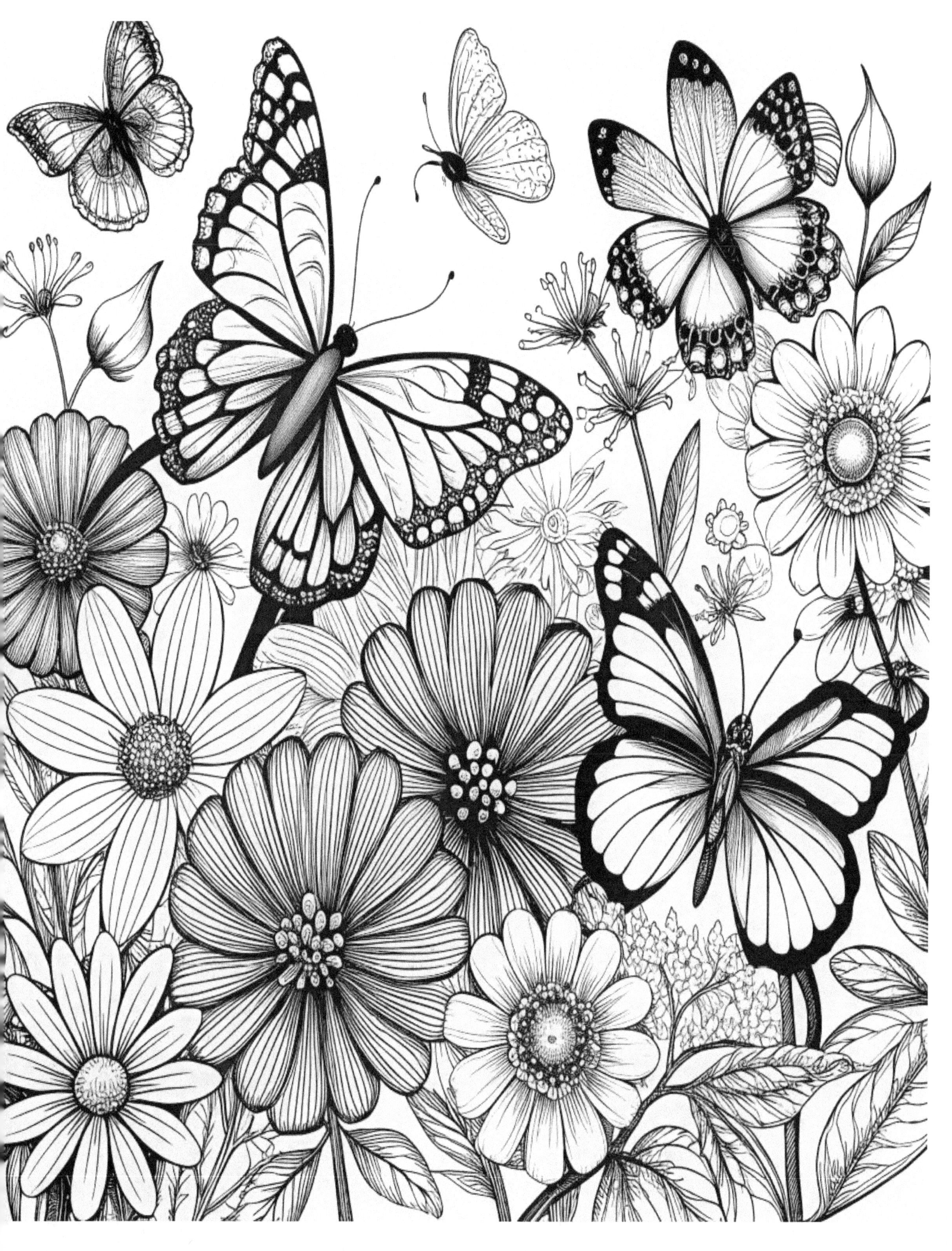

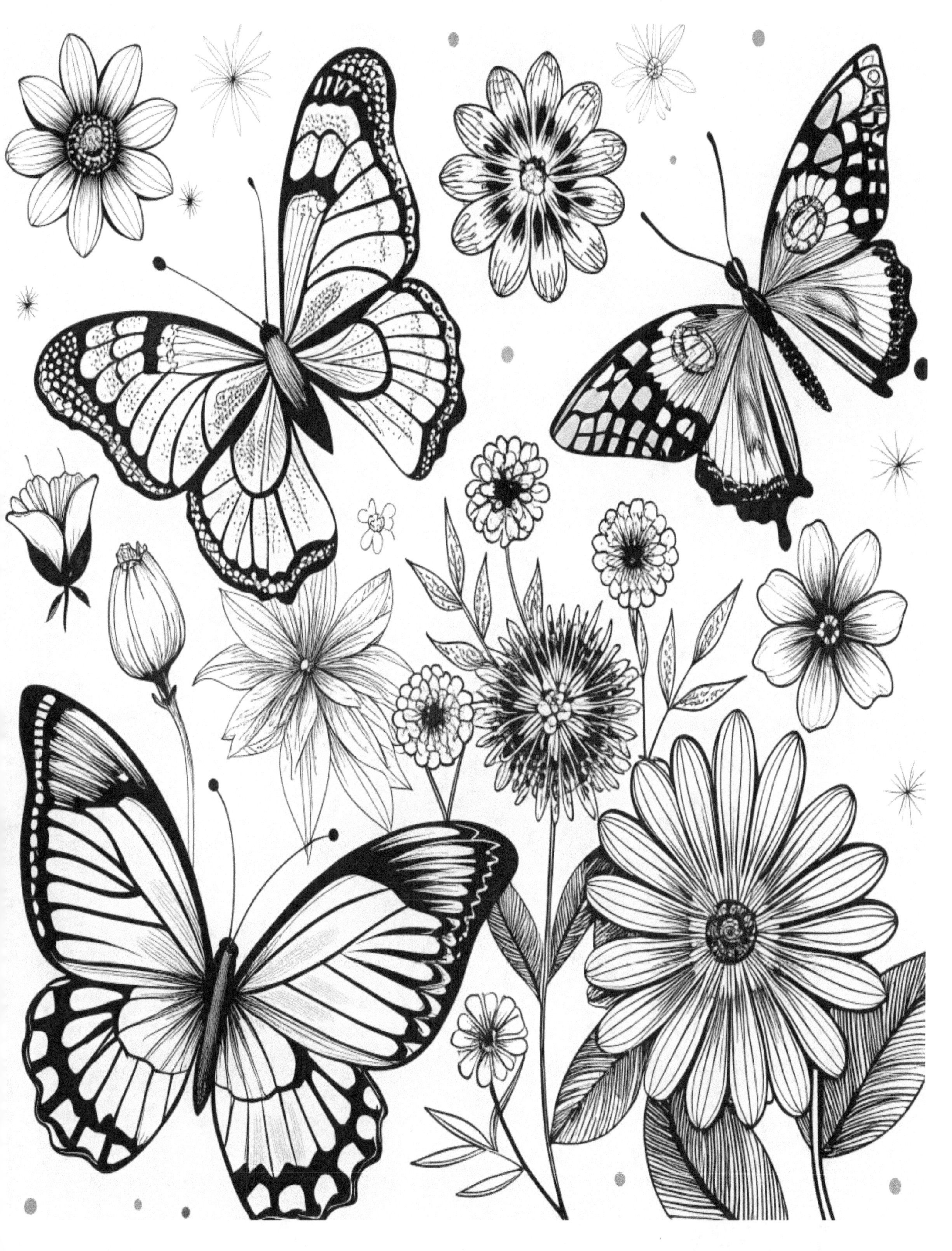

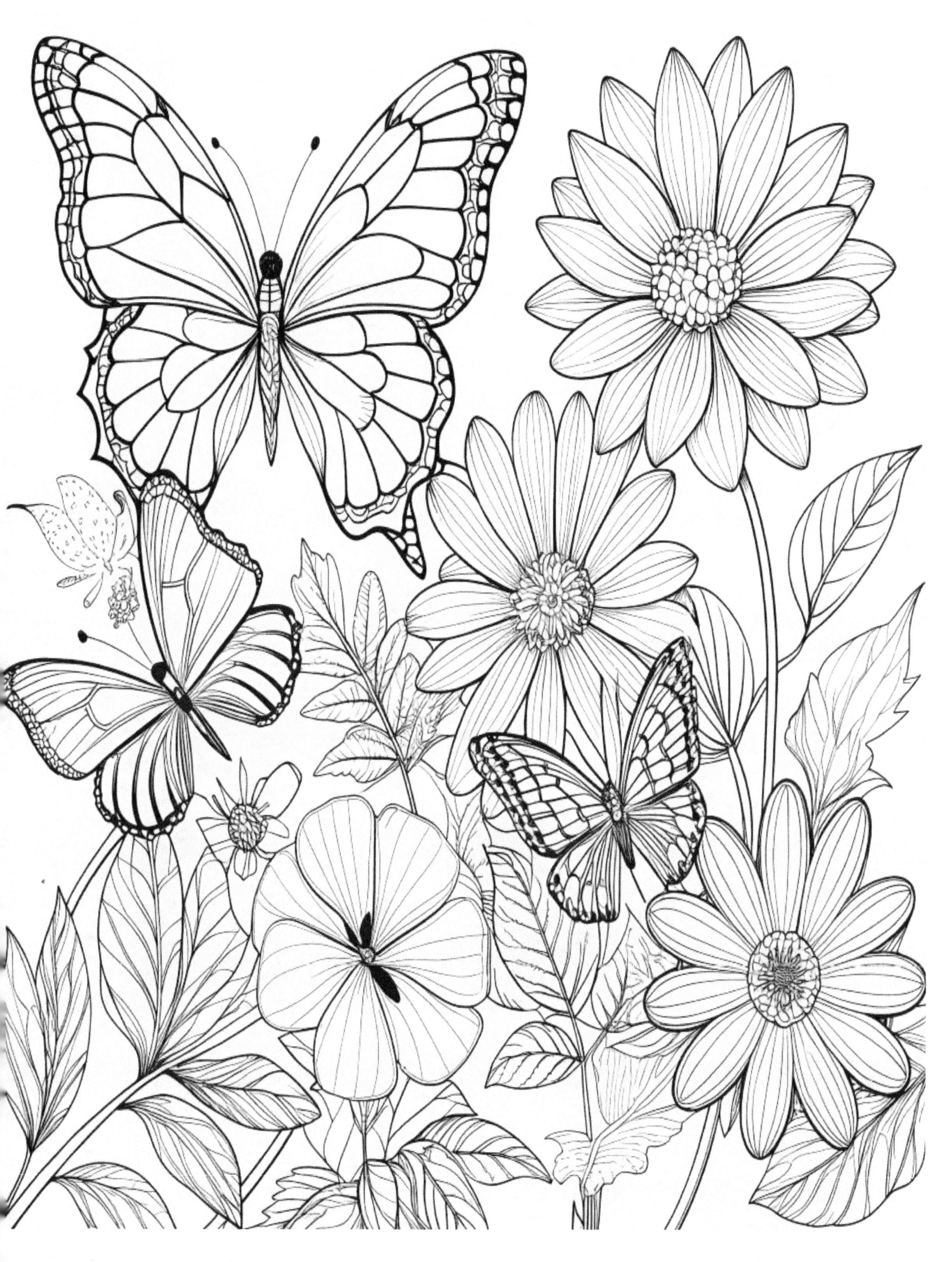

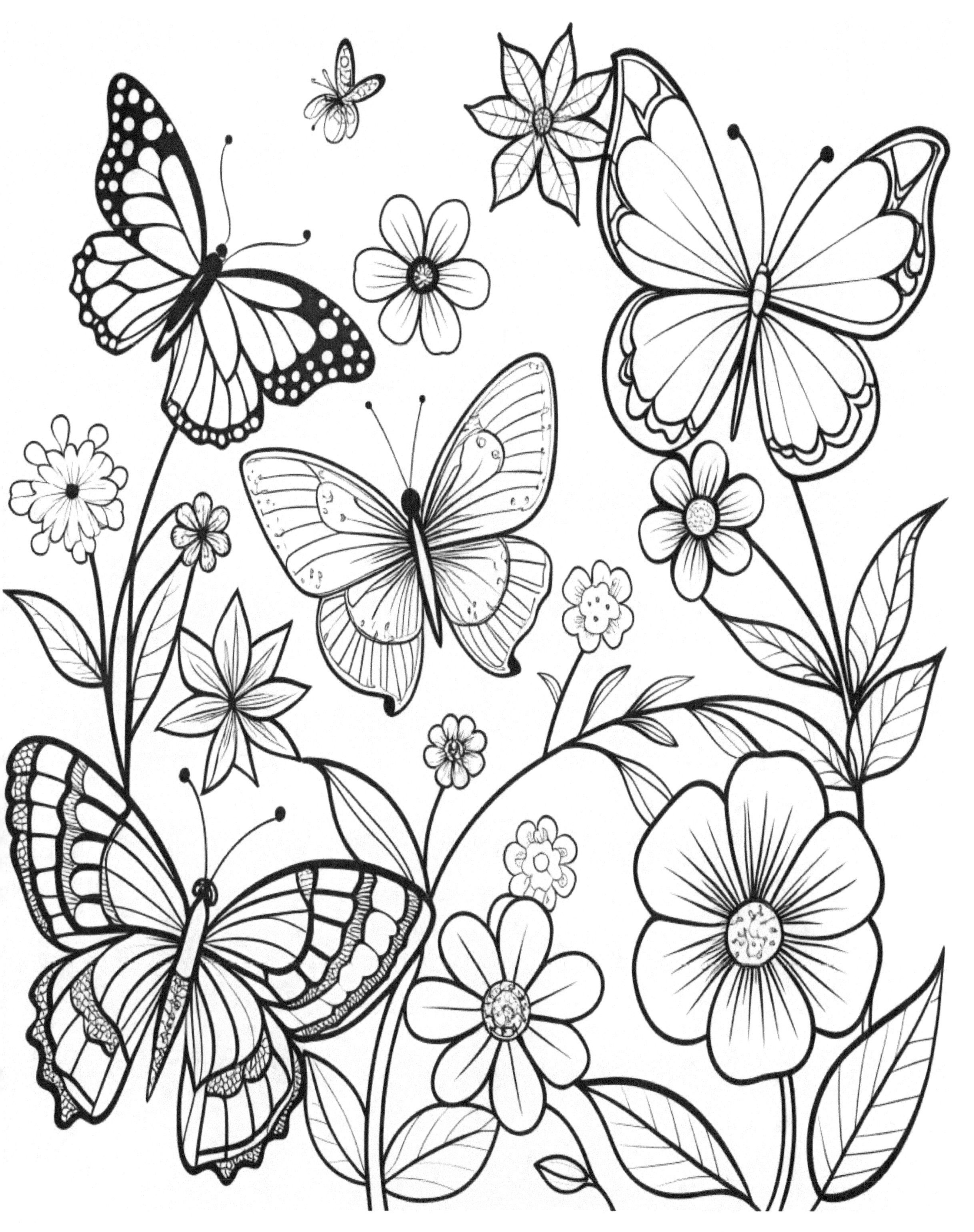

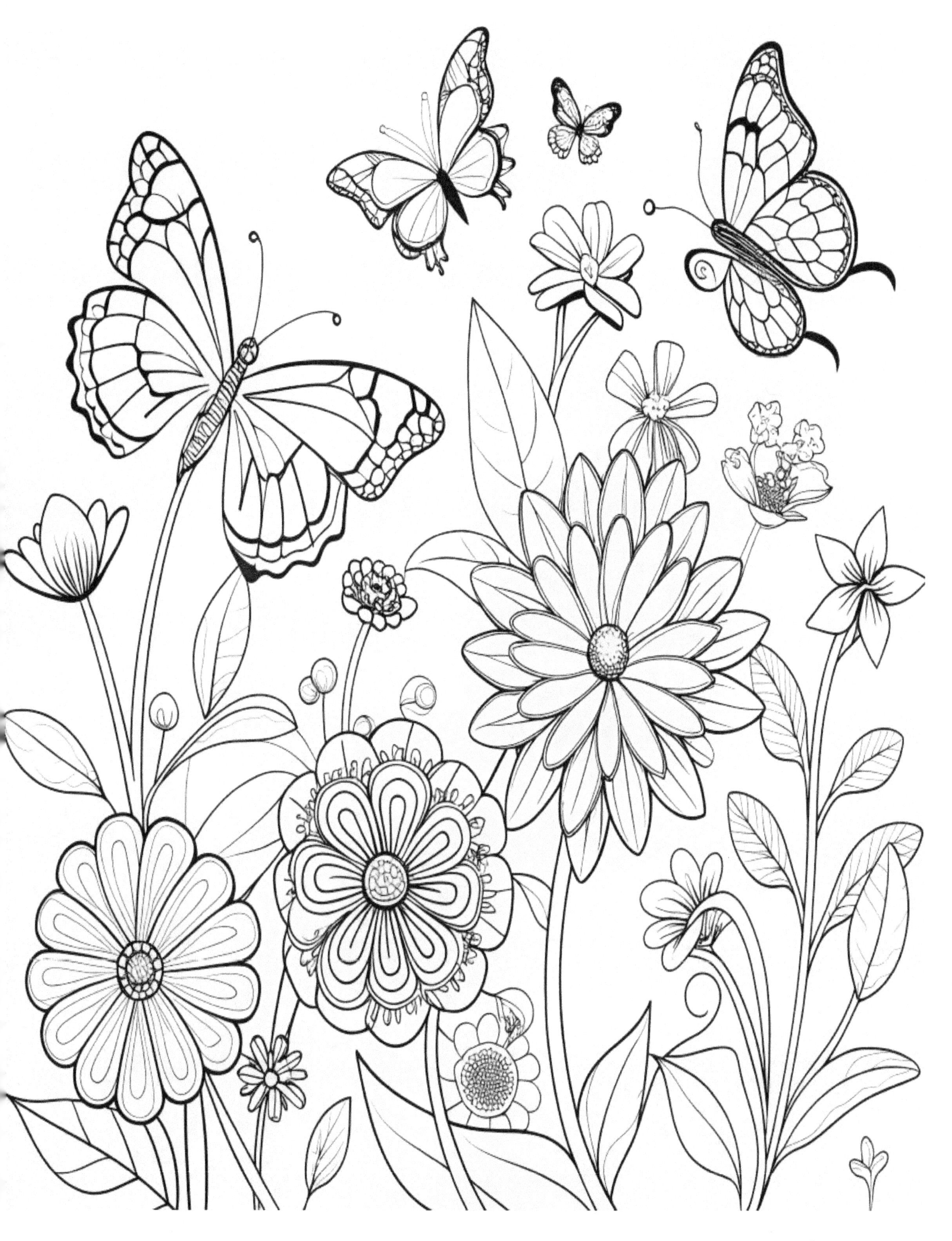

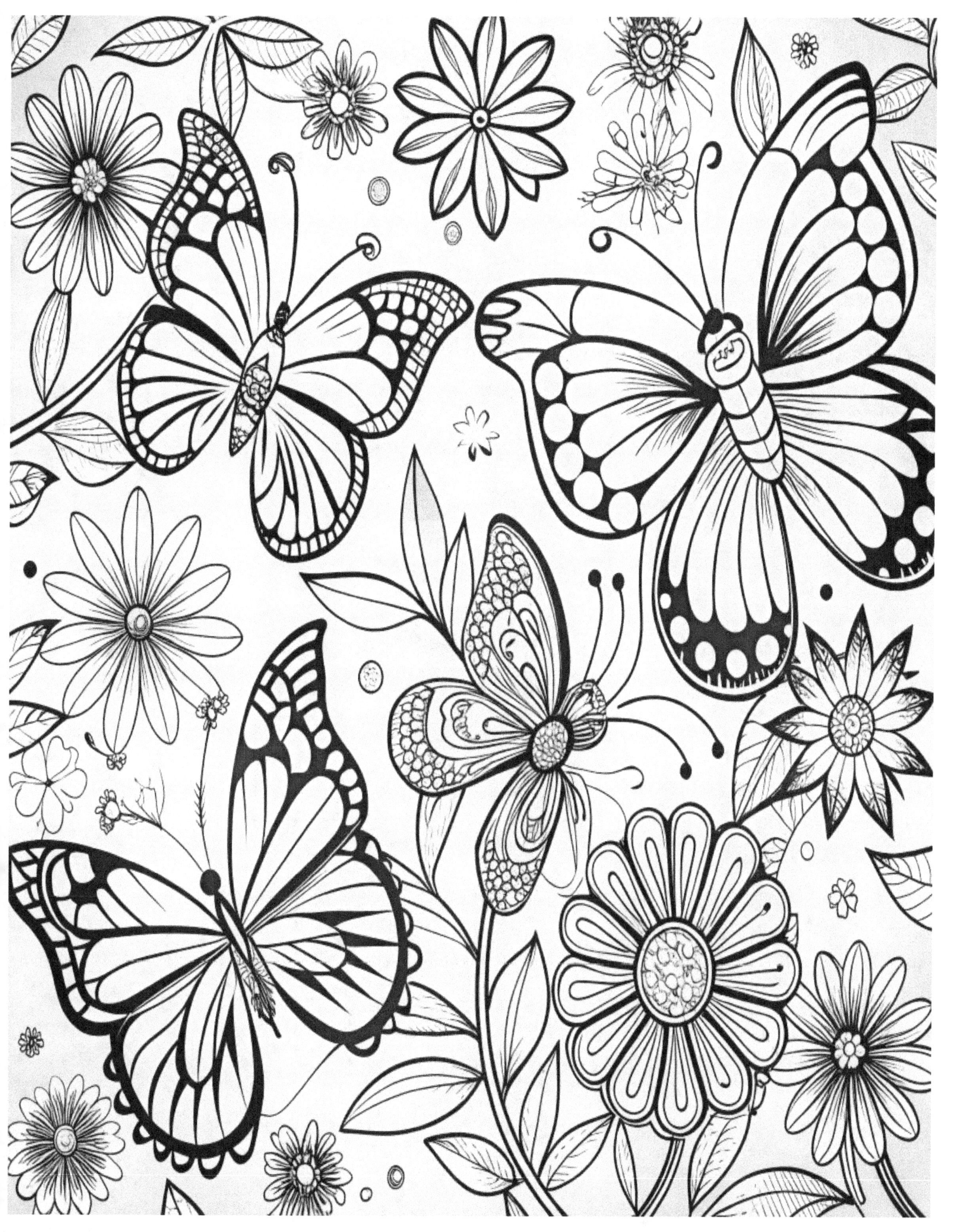

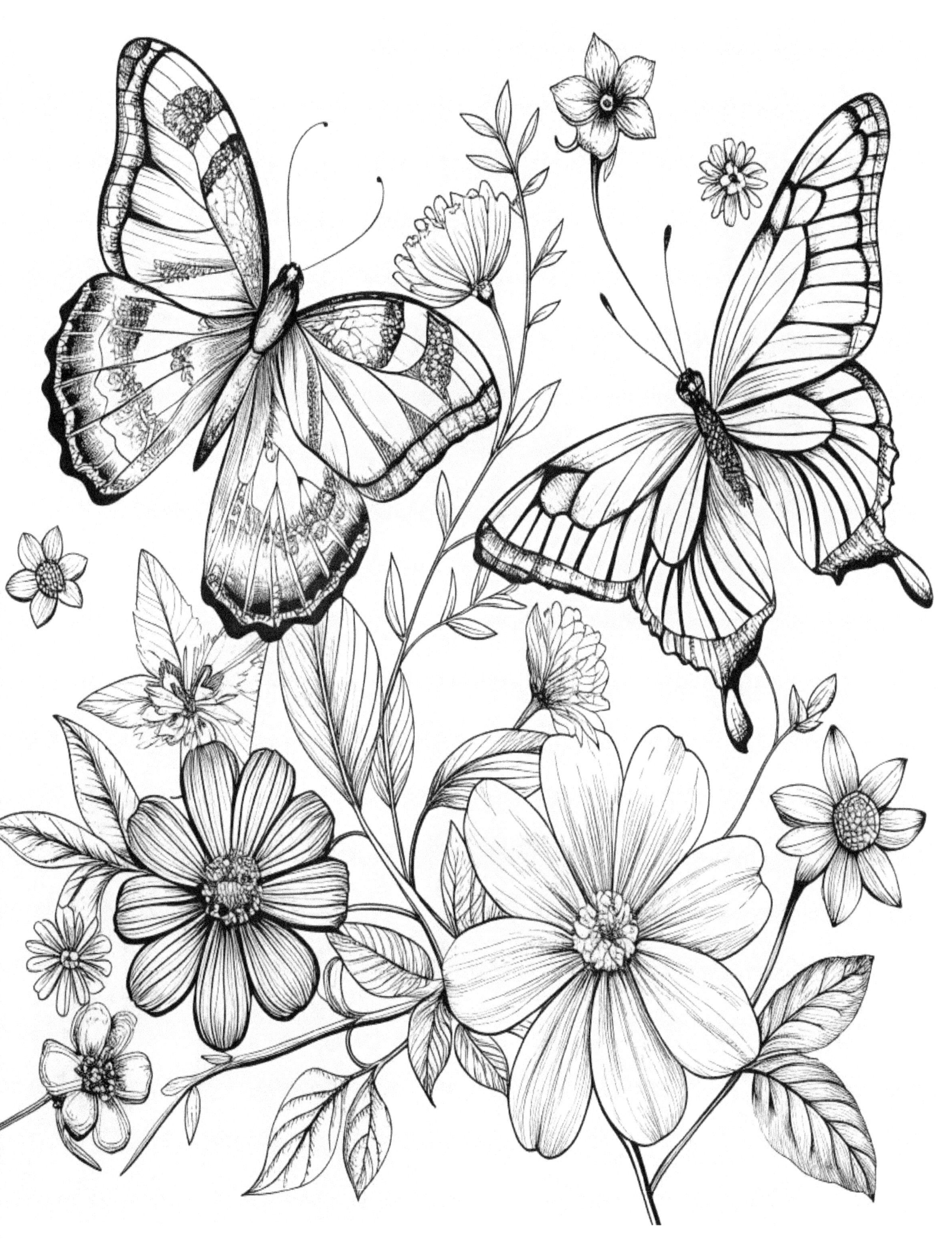

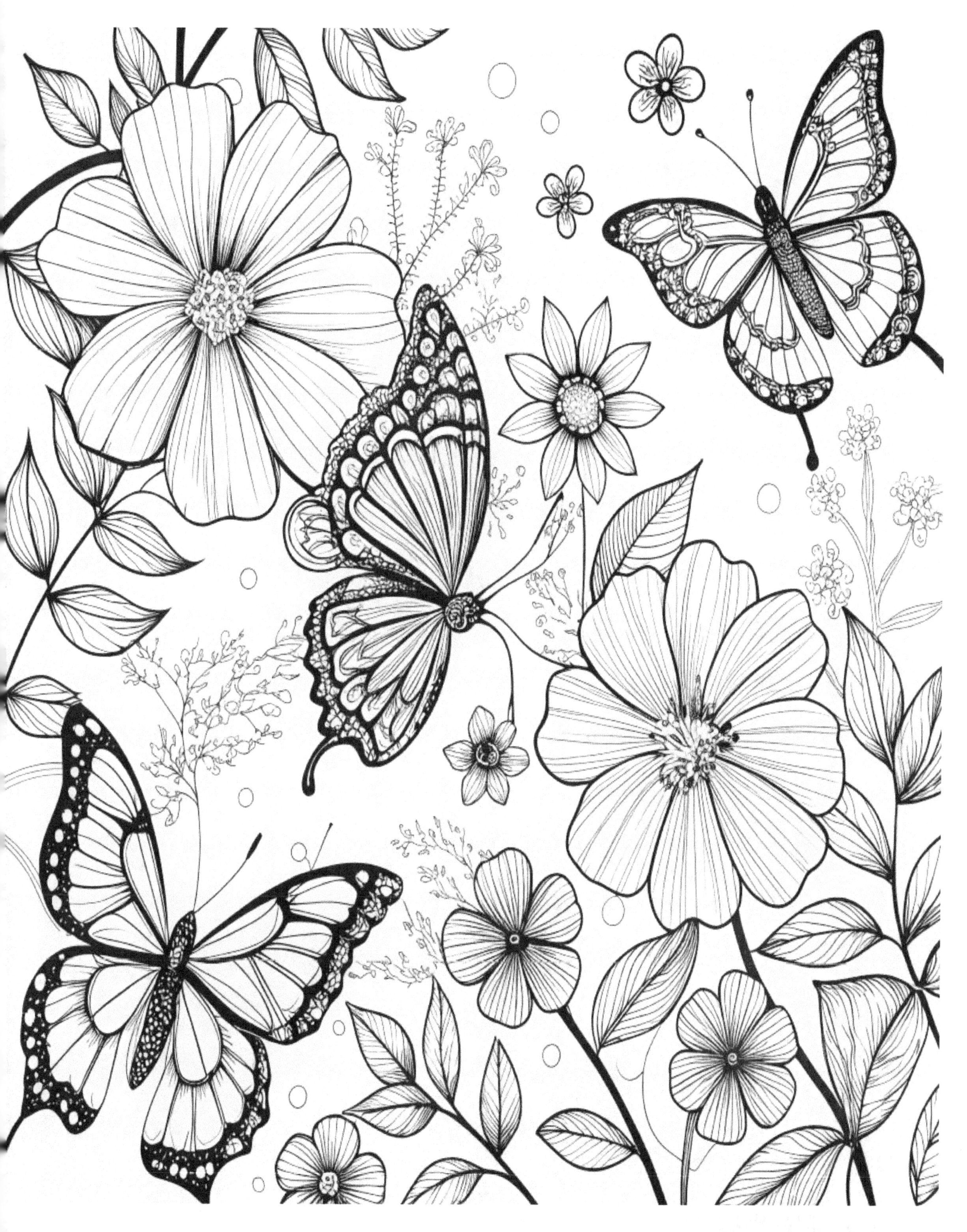

www.ingramcontent.com/pod-product-compliance
Lightning Source LLC
Chambersburg PA
CBHW081957260726
48659CB00009BA/2957

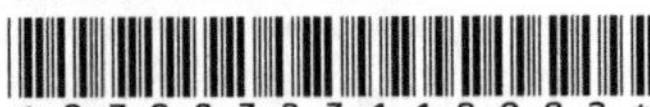